THE
BURMESE
KITCHEN

ALSO BY COPELAND MARKS

The Varied Kitchens of India

False Tongues and Sunday Bread
a Guatemalan and Mayan Cookbook

The Indonesian Cookbook
(with Mintart Soeharjo)

THE
BURMESE
KITCHEN

COPELAND MARKS
AND AUNG THEIN

M. Evans and Company, Inc.
New York

Library of Congress Cataloging-in-Publication Data

Marks, Copeland.
  The Burmese kitchen.

  Bibliography: p.
  Includes index.
  1. Cookery, Burmese. I. Thein, Aung. II. Title.
TX724.5.B93M37 1987   641.59591   87-22242

ISBN 0-87131-524-6

M. Evans and Company, Inc.
216 East 49 Street
New York, New York 10017

Design by Lauren Dong

Manufactured in the United States of America

9 8 7 6 5 4 3 2 1

CONTENTS

TX
724.5
.B93
m37
1989

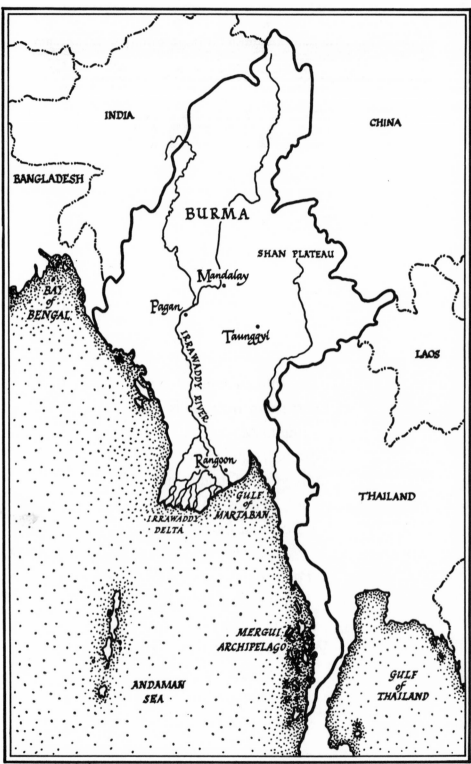

INDIA

CHINA

BANGLADESH

BAY
of
BENGAL

BURMA

SHAN PLATEAU

Mandalay

Pagan

Taunggyi

LAOS

IRRAWADDY RIVER

Rangoon

GULF
of
MARTABAN

THAILAND

IRRAWADDY
DELTA

MERGUI
ARCHIPELAGO

ANDAMAN
SEA

GULF
of
THAILAND

STAUB

INTRODUCTION

"The Burmans are not Indian, nor are they Chinese," says W. S. Desai in his book *India and Burma.* "They are a people with a distinct nationality of their own, developed during a history of over one thousand years. During this period they created a political and social system of their own. Their civilization is distinctly 'Burmese,' with their own language, literature, art, even though highly influenced by India and China, and more deeply so by the former." It is this succinct statement that defines a unique people, the Burmese, and nowhere is this shown so well as in their cuisine. To define the basic characteristics of a little-known cuisine, one must take on the cloak of a detective and gather clues. They are everywhere waiting to be documented and are observable here as a reflection of the Burmese history and religion as well as of their geography and agriculture.

The Burmese nation is reputed to have started about 2,500 years ago with a series of population movements, from Central Asia and the China-Tibetan region, into what is now Burma. The peoples and the languages they spoke were the beginnings of this unique culture. Local kings and kingdoms rose, lost power, and fell; the Portuguese emigrated from Goa, their colony on India's western coast, to form a settlement; and finally, during the 1800s and after years of battling, England annexed Burma to British India. Burma won its independence in 1948 (after having been occupied by the Japanese during World War II) and became a socialist republic in 1974.

Rangoon, now the largest city, was a fishing village until 1753 when it was made the capital. Mandalay ("where the flying fishes play") is the second city and was established in 1859. In our minds, both cities are the epitome of romance and exotic mysticism, thanks to the writings of such authors as Rudyard Kipling and Noel Coward. However, with the coming of British rule, much of the romance fled, leaving British economy the real ruler.

The old religion was based on the worship of spirits, called Nats, each one of which was responsible for a particular area of life. During the very early years, Buddhism became widespread and has ever since exerted the most profound influence over all that is Burmese. Today the vast majority of the population are Buddhists. Large numbers have joined religious orders and are connected to pagodas or monasteries, where they meditate in pursuit of enlightenment. Intertwined with the Buddhist religion is the old religion of the spirits, and Buddhists still acknowledge their household gods.

The Buddhists have a prohibition against killing any animals but no prohibition against eating meat, so they depend on Muslim and Chinese butchers. The Muslims will not touch pork but will kill and eat other meats. The Chinese are the pork (and chicken) butchers in Burma, and are also known as enthusiastic pork-eaters—hence the many delicious and distinctive pork recipes. Although meat eating is not generally forbidden, these restrictions, as well as the availability of fresh fruits and vegetables year-round, result in a cuisine rich with vegetarian recipes.

Burma's boundaries touch upon those of two culinary giants: India and China. Their southeastern neighbor, Thailand, also exerts an influence that cannot be discounted. The spices and cooking methods of all three are evident in these recipes. Here, as elsewhere, regional preferences and availability of foodstuffs influence the individual style. The mountainous areas, far from the ocean, utilize meat and poultry but hardly any fish, except that which is dried. On its western border Burma faces the sea, and its interior is irrigated by an enormous chain of rivers, particularly the Irrawaddy. Freshwater fish and seafood in all its ramifications is in plentiful supply in these areas. The seaports produce the freshest, finest prawns, lobster, and fish, which are then cooked in the style of the region; there is a plethora of recipes for both fresh and dried fish, in particular for dried shrimps, which are ubiquitous and indispensable. Nowhere else have I been served such an eye-popping variety of incomparable dishes of seafood—incomparable mostly because of the speed with which the main ingredient moves from the fisherman to the table.

Rice is perhaps the next most important staple; it is eaten at every meal. Agricultural produce grown on a soil of undiminished fertility once made Burma the world's largest exporter of rice, and rice is still produced in great quantity. I have seen and tasted the black and pink rice of Upper Burma as well as many other varieties and grades of this remarkable grain.

That isn't all. Nature has lavished on the country an unlimited variety of botanical edibles. On a drive through the countryside— green, lush, and tranquil—it appears as though everything that grows is edible. Aquatic plants growing in and along the streams, trees heavy with fruit, and long stretches of rice plantings fill the eye. The Burmese have a natural liking for green leaves and vines in their salads and soups; they utilize everything.

Spices and condiments are of primary importance to the cuisine. The indispensable fish sauce (*nam pya ye*), shrimp paste (*ngappi*), soy sauce, and the triumvirate of garlic, ginger, and turmeric, reveal the influence of India and China. Cuminseed, coriander, paprika (for color), and hot chilies are used generously, and all is lubricated with coconut milk.

Besan (chick-pea flour) is incorporated in salads. Salads so complex we would call them one-dish meals are the hallmark of Burmese cooking—whether it be Rangoon, Mandalay, small agricultural towns, or the tribal regions of the Shan, Karen, and Kachin. The glory of the cuisine is the variety of these one-dish preparations; a platter of noodles and sauce, embellished with a number of unusual garnishes and side dishes, becomes a production. An elaborate example of this is the famous Mandalay Mishee (see Index), which is considered a noodle salad but includes, in addition to noodles, pork fritter, tofu puffs, and three kinds of sauce. Or the Dan Bauk (Chicken and Rice, see Index) served with onion, pepper, and fresh mint salad. Technically none of these preparations is demanding, but they do require a number of steps and a variety of ingredients to keep them traditional.

Soup is not a separate course but is served throughout the meal in place of tea, coffee, or other beverage. It may seem curious that, in a hot tropical climate, one is served so many soups. But these light soups, prepared with greens such as sorrel, spinach, or aquatic leaves, are served at room temperature—not hot, like the winter soups of temperate climates.

So the clues have been collected but the result can be known only by tasting as many different dishes as possible—at home, in a restaurant, or in Burma itself.

Our aim in this volume is to introduce the Burmese style of cooking to the American public. Here are recipes and directions to start you on the way. We hope it will persuade you that this cuisine deserves the popularity that has so far eluded it in the American kitchen.

GLOSSARY OF INGREDIENTS

AGAR-AGAR (*Porphyra umbilicalis*): A colorless derivative from a sea-weed, dried and packaged in strings or pieces. Used as a substitute for gelatin to solidify desserts. Available here in Asian food markets.

BAMBOO SHOOTS (*Bambusa vulgaris*): The shoots of the bamboo plant, which springs up during monsoon rains, are widely used throughout Asia. Canned bamboo shoots of several different varieties are available in Asian food shops.

SOUR BAMBOO SHOOTS: These shoots are sliced thin, in pieces about 1 inch square, and preserved in salt, water, and vinegar. They are mildly fermented, slightly sour, and highly compatible with pork. The Globe brand, canned in Taiwan, is available in a 1-pound, 3-ounce size or a 14-ounce plastic package.

BEAN PASTE: A slightly sweet purée prepared from soybeans and available in Oriental food shops. The brand I use is the Koon Chun brand from Hong Kong.

BEAN SPROUTS: Used freely in the Burmese diet, mung bean sprouts are available fresh in specialty shops and supermarkets.

BESAN: This is flour derived from the chick-pea (*Cicer arietinum*). It is also called *gram* and is one of the ubiquitous pulses of India. *Besan* is used frequently in Burmese cooking, but it must be considered a culinary import from India. The Burmese use *besan* with great ingenuity as a toasted seasoning in salads and as a thickener in the famous On No Kyauk Swe (Chicken Curry with Coconut Milk Gravy, see Index).

BITTER MELON *(Momordica charantia)*: A beautifully sculptured gourd, a cucumberlike vegetable with a bitter taste that can become habit-forming. It is eaten with gusto in Burma, India, and Indonesia. When combined with other strong flavorings such as ginger, garlic, fish sauce, and dried chilies, as in Kyethinga (Shrimp-Flavored Bitter Melon, see Index), the bitterness is mitigated.

BLACK GRAM *(Phaseolus mungo)*: The *urd dhal*, a popular tropical pulse crop of South India.

BOTTLE GOURD: See GOURDS.

CALABASH *(Benincasa hispida)*: Also called "fuzzy melon," this is a cucumber-shaped gourd. It has the same texture and flavor as the Bottle Gourd.

CHAYOTE *(Sechium edule)*: A Central American pear-shaped squashlike vegetable that I first encountered during my many years of working in Guatemala. To see it piled high in the markets of Burma (along with avocado) was a revelation. That made apparent how rapidly agricultural products move from one continent to another, and are accepted and integrated into a new culinary mainstream.

CHILI *(Capsicum frutescens)*: Reams of material have been written about this plant, whose botanical origin was in Central America. It spread rapidly over the rest of the world in the fifteenth century when the Spanish took it to Europe after the Conquest of Central and South America. The semihot chili that the Burmese use is also called "elephant trunk" in India since that is what it resembles. It is available in specialty shops as well as in supermarkets that cater to Latin and Asian communities. Hot chili is utilized both fresh and dried (red chili flakes) in Burmese food and is so all-pervasive that the cuisine is unthinkable without it.

COCONUT MILK, COCONUT CREAM: See How to Make chapter.

CORIANDER *(Coriandrum sativum)*: A most popular fresh garnish in Burmese cooking. This almost universal aromatic herb is found all over Asia, and I have used it frequently in Guatemala for Central American dishes as well. Dried coriander, whole seeds and ground, is a kitchen staple in Burmese cooking and untold others.

DAY LILY BUDS *(Hemerocallis fulva)*: Also known as "golden needles," they are available in Asian markets. They are soaked in hot water and then tied in knots so that they do not disintegrate during cooking.

DRIED BEAN CURD *(Yuba)*: This is available in two types; one is small flat sheets and the other is twisted ropes about 12 inches in length.

DRIED SHRIMP: One of the staples in a Burmese kitchen—both whole tiny shrimps and shrimp powder. A trip through Scott's Market in Rangoon, the great central market of the city, is an eye opener. Mounds of dried shrimps in various sizes and shades of pink/orange greet eager buyers. They are an indispensable flavoring in soups and salads.

Dried SHRIMP POWDER is simply dried shrimps ground to a powder in a food processor. The powder is used in salads and other dishes.

FERMENTED TEA LEAVES: see Index.

FISH SAUCE: *Nam pya ye* in Burmese, this bottled extract of anchovy is indispensable. The Tiparos brand from Thailand is very good, and there are several others that are equally authentic. Fish sauce is to the Burmese what soy sauce is to the Chinese.

GARAM MASALA: Literally, "hot spice," of Indian origin. It is a combination of ground spices that might include cloves, cinnamon, pepper, cardamom, and cuminseed, among others.

GINGER *(Zingiber officinale)*: In the cooking of Burma this refers exclusively to fresh gingerroot. The rhizomes covered with a thin tan-colored skin are found in Asian markets and many supermarkets. The young gingerroot, which has a light pink cast, is grown in Hawaii and used in fresh ginger salads (see Index). The juice squeezed from slices of ginger is also an effective flavoring.

GLUTINOUS RICE: See RICE.

GOURDS: Tropical gourds are one of those ubiquitous sights in tropical Asia where the vines grow luxuriously over fences, decaying colonial mansions, or the roofs of peasant huts and hovels. Gourds are an easy and always available source of vegetable.

BOTTLE GOURD *(Lagenaria siceraria)*, also known as Indian gourd, a green squash shaped like a slim-necked bottle. Young gourds are the tastiest.

RIDGE GOURD *(Luffa acutangula)* is a long green cylinder with pointed ends. Ridges about ¼ inch high run the length of the gourd, and these are peeled off. The flesh and seeds have a texture similar to tender cucumbers. The dried ridge gourd is known as "luffa" and is used as a bath sponge.

SNAKE GOURD (*Trichosanthes cucumerina*), also known as long gourd, is a long green twisting tube, snakelike, therefore its name. In Calcutta, the snake gourd is also known as snake oil, the reason for which I have been unable to learn. The gourds grow on vines held above ground on a trellis arrangement. Gourds are encouraged to grow downward, helped along by having a small stone tied onto the end, allowing gravity to pull the gourd straight as it grows. Some of the gourds grow up to six feet in length. The gourd itself has an empty cylinder in the center and lends itself to being stuffed as in Pelinmwe (Stuffed Snake Gourd, see Index).

Gourds are found mainly in Asian vegetable markets, especially New York's Chinatown, where a large Asian population has created a continuous demand.

JAGGERY: see PALM SUGAR.

JAPANESE RADISH: see WHITE RADISH.

LEMONGRASS (*Cymbopogon citratus*): A distinctive and popular flavoring in the kitchens of Burma, Thailand, and Indonesia. It is a pleasure to report that it is available from the sidewalk merchants in New York's Chinatown. The long, lemon-scented stalks are frequently used in soups and curries.

LEPHET: Fermented tea leaves; see Index for recipe.

LONG BEANS (*Vigna unguiculata*, subsp. *sesquipedalis*): Also known as Chinese long beans, these grow 16 inches or more in length. A tender narrow bean, available in Chinatown and in some specialty produce markets.

NOODLES: Rice may be the staff of life in Burma but it is noodles that stick to the ribs. This was brought out to me forcefully one early morning in Rangoon as I was foraging for breakfast rather than have the conventional Western breakfast in the hotel. As long as the pot bubbles, I have no qualms about eating in small roadside stands. There one finds trestle tables, low wood tools, and a tarpaulin or wood covering to serve as a roof in the event of a sudden tropical downpour. The Waldorf-Astoria it isn't.

FRESH EGG NOODLES, Chinese-style, are used in Mohinga (Classic Fish Soup, see Index). They are cooked *al dente* and included as part of the recipe. Chinatown grocers will usually stock egg noodles of several sizes from the very thin to the same size as No. 9 supermarket spaghetti.

RICE NOODLES, RICE STICKS, RICE VERMICELLI are all the same. They are noodles of various sizes or thicknesses made of rice, water, and salt. The packages that I have are imported from Thailand, Taiwan, or China. Some of the packages marked "rice sticks" are very thin, almost hairlike and white. Other rice sticks are from ¼ inch to 1 inch wide like the ones used in Mandalay Nangyi (Rice Noodle Salad, see Index). They should be presoaked in warm water from 5 to 10 minutes to soften. The name "rice vermicelli" usually refers to thin rice noodles.

Round RICE SHEETS are made and sold fresh; they are white and flexible. Available in Chinatown factories and shops. They are also known as "Malay noodles" in Burma, which could indicate their origin. The rice sheet should be used and eaten the day of purchase. Refrigeration makes it stiff as a board and it requires steaming to soften to its original state.

CELLOPHANE NOODLES are made from the mung beans (*Phaseolus aureus*) known as "green gram." They originate in India. It is this bean from which bean sprouts are germinated. The cellophane noodle is a very fine translucent thread, dried and sold in small packets weighing about 2 ounces. The noodle is soaked in warm water for 5 minutes to soften before using.

PALM SUGAR (derived from the Sugar Palm, *Arenga saccharifera*): Known as "jaggery" in India, it has an intense, sweet caramel flavor similar but superior to commercial brown sugar, which may serve as a substitute albeit an inadequate one.

PEPYOAT: This is an ingredient in Burmese recipes made by sprouting and cooking dried garden peas (known as *vatana* in Indian food shops). (See Index.)

RED LENTIL (*Lens culinaris*): Also called "Egyptian lentil." It is a deep orange color, quite small, with high protein content, and altogether delicious when combined with rice or used in soups.

RICE (*Oryza sativa*): Although there are many varieties of rice grown and used in Burma (see Index), it is the regular long-grain rice that is a staple in the daily diet. In these recipes, regular rice should be used unless glutinous (short-grain) rice is specifically called for. Glutinous rice (also known as sweet or sticky rice) is used in preparing sweets, and both rice flour and glutinous rice flour are used to make up batters and snacks. All are available in Asian markets or specialty food shops.

RICE NOODLES, RICE SHEETS: See NOODLES.

SHRIMP PASTE: Called *pazun ngapi* in Burmese, it is a bottled concentrate of shrimp, thick and pungent. Used in moderate amounts, it develops depth in sauces, meat, poultry, and fish. Shrimp paste, imported from Hong Kong and Thailand, is available in Asian food shops. The bottle presently in my refrigerator is from Hong Kong.

SNAKE GOURD: see GOURDS.

SOYBEAN CURD: see TOFU.

STAR ANISE (*Illicium verum*): A native of China, related to the magnolia tree, not to the anise of Western cooking. Its distinctive flavor is used now and then in Burmese cooking.

TAMARIND PASTE: From the pod of the tamarind tree (*Tamarindus indica*). The paste is diluted in water and strained, then added to sauces, dips, and an assortment of curries. Its characteristic acid taste has found favor all over the Asian tropics and Central America. It is found in Southeast Asian food shops and some Latin American stores, pressed into packages with the seeds and bits of stems. The ones I use are imported from Thailand and Singapore.

TARO ROOT (*Colocasia esculenta*): A starchy, potatolike tuber utilized by the Burmese to prepare a stuffed cutlet, Peinu Asathut (see Index).

TOFU: The Chinese name for soybean curd is used in these pages and by the Burmese. The Chinese style is the firm variety of soybean cake, which can be deep-fried to crispness and is often treated this way. The Japanese style is thick, with a creamy consistency, and is preferred for soups. Both types have become so common in American food emporiums that they have lost their exotic reputation. They are used with some frequency in Burmese cooking.

TOHU: Like tofu, but prepared with gram or chick-peas rather than soybeans and exclusively Burmese (see How to Make chapter).

TURMERIC (*Curcuma longa*): This rhizome has a very special place in the galaxy of Burmese spices. Use of ⅛ teaspoon here and there in the cooking oil imparts a moderate flavor but a distinctive yellow color. Used in curries and condiments in moderate amounts, it turns up everywhere in the cooking. Turmeric is the principal coloring ingredient in Indian curry powders.

WATER SPINACH *(Ipomoea aquatica)*: A delicate plant with arrow-shaped leaves and hollow stems.

WHITE RADISH *(Raphanus sativus)*: Also known as Chinese or Japanese radish *(daikon* in Japan). Large, long, and thick radishes, which are conspicuous in Chinatown vegetable stands. Eaten both cooked and raw.

WINTER MELON *(Benincasa hispida)*: Also called ash pumpkin by the Chinese since at maturity it is covered by a white dust. The crisp, white pulp is covered by a hard, green skin; the pumpkin sometimes grows to 25 pounds. It is used in soups and curry. In New York's Chinatown, the melon is sold by the pound, cut into pieces.

HOW TO MAKE...

SPICY BATTER FOR FRIED VEGETABLES

⅔ cup rice flour
3 tablespoons glutinous rice flour
2 tablespoons chick-pea flour (besan)
½ teaspoon baking powder
⅛ teaspoon ground turmeric
⅛ teaspoon paprika
1 garlic clove, chopped fine
1 teaspoon fine-chopped fresh ginger
1 tablespoon corn or peanut oil
½ cup cold water

Mix everything together and let stand, refrigerated, for 1 hour or more before using. When prepared like this in advance (notice it does not have salt in it to make the vegetables turn soggy), the fritters develop a crisp texture.

MAKES ABOUT 1½ CUPS

PAGAN PONYEE GYI

Fermented Black Bean Paste

2 pounds black turtle beans, rinsed
9 cups water
1 teaspoon salt

1. Put beans, water, and salt into a large pan and bring to a boil over moderate heat. Cook for about 1 hour, or until about 3 cups of liquid remain. Strain liquid into a glass or pottery bowl, not into metal or plastic.

Do this twice more, using the same beans and another 9 cups water (no salt). Bring to a boil and cook until 3 cups liquid remain; strain. At the end of the third time around you will have 9 cups strained, black liquid.

2. Cover this liquid with glass or clear plastic to allow light to penetrate and let it ferment in a sunny window for 3 days. At the end of 3 days you will notice a thick, firm black top has formed.

3. Smooth the thick top into the fermented liquid and cook in a metal pan over moderate heat for about 1 hour to evaporate nearly all the liquid. Stir constantly. Reduce heat to low and stir the porridge for 15 minutes more as the paste thickens. Large bubbles form and break, spattering (and burning) anything nearby, so be very careful at this stage.

4. Cool the paste, put it into a glass jar with a cover, and back in a sunny window for 3 days to ferment further.

You will then have a fermented black bean paste to use in several recipes.

The cooked whole black beans that remain are reserved for another use.

MAKES ABOUT 3 CUPS

TOHU

Burmese Bean Curd

3 cups chick-pea flour (besan)
15 cups water
1 teaspoon corn or peanut oil
¼ teaspoon ground turmeric
1 teaspoon salt

1. Mix the chick-pea flour and water together with a whisk or egg beater. Let stand overnight, about 12 hours.

2. Next day, strain the mixture, one quarter at a time, through a thin cotton cloth. Help the mixture through the cloth by stirring and pressing. Scrape out the residue from the cloth and discard it. Let the balance of the liquid settle for 3 hours.

3. With a soup ladle carefully remove 6 cups of liquid from the top of the mixture without disturbing the balance. Discard the 6 cups liquid you have removed.

4. Rub the bottom of a large pan with the oil. Pour in *almost all* of the balance of the liquid (9 cups) and add the turmeric and salt. What remains in the original pan is a thick chick-pea sludge, about 1 cup. This should be reserved in a bowl for future use.

5. Bring to a boil the 9 cups of liquid and cook over moderate heat for 30 minutes, stirring continuously. At this time, add the chick-pea sludge, which is a thickening agent, and continue to cook over low heat for 10 minutes more, stirring the thick mixture firmly. Remove the pan from the heat.

6. Turn out the mixture into a tray 12 × 4 inches and 3 inches deep, lined with a clean cotton cloth. Cool completely, uncovered, overnight. At this stage you may slice the firm *tohu* into pieces of whatever size you wish. It is ready to use.

MAKES 6 CUPS

BESAN

Toasted Chick-Pea Flour

½ cup chick-pea flour

Put the chick-pea flour in a dry skillet (a pan with nonstick lining works well) and stir continuously over moderately low heat until the flour turns a light tan or coffee color. Do not scorch. Cool. Store in a jar with a tight cover on the kitchen shelf for future use.

COCONUT MILK

1 ripe coconut, with brown, hard shell
4 to 5 cups very hot water

1. Bake the coconut in a 400°F. oven for 15 to 20 minutes; a little more will not harm. Remove coconut from oven and give it several hard whacks with a hammer to break it open and into 4 or 5 pieces. The coconut *water* is not used and will drain away.

2. Pry the coconut meat from the shell with a dull knife, to eliminate the possibility of running the knife through one's fingers. Cut the meat into 1-inch-wide strips and then into horizontal thin slices.

3. Put about 3 cups of the slices into a blender container and pour in 4 cups of water (the less water, the richer the coconut milk). Process for about 1 minute, which will be enough time to cut up the coconut and release the milk. Pour the mixture through a metal sieve, squeeze out the coconut fragments and discard. The liquid that remains is coconut milk. It can be stored in the refrigerator for 3 days, or it can be frozen in plastic containers for future use.

SUGARED COCONUT
To make this, toss 1 cup coconut flakes with 1 tablespoon sugar.

Note: For canned coconut milk, we recommend the TC brand from Thailand. It is a thick, natural coconut milk without sweetening; it may be used in meat and fish dishes as well as desserts.

COCONUT MILK AND COCONUT CREAM, BURMESE STYLE

Strictly for information purposes, we are including the Burmese method of making coconut milk. Interesting to read about but dangerous to undertake!

2 coconuts, with brown husk
1 hand grater and stand
1 teaspoon salt
3 cups warm (tepid) water
1 wet cotton kitchen towel

1. Scrape off the outside fibers of the coconuts, in effect, giving them a shave. Rinse off the outside so that fragments do not fall into the grated coconut.

2. Hold the coconut in your palm. Take a meat cleaver (not a hammer) and crack the center hard. Turn the coconut 2 inches more and crack the center again. The coconut will usually split into halves.

3. Using a village coconut scraper, rub the inside of the coconut halves lightly against the scraper (which is attached to a wooden stand) until all the coconut has been scraped away. Put the grated coconut, about 6 cups for both coconuts, into a large bowl.

4. Pour 1 cup water over the grated coconut. Sprinkle the salt over. Mix, mash, and squeeze the coconut with your hands to extract the milk. Take a large handful of the coconut and squeeze it firmly into the kitchen cloth draped over a bowl. Squeeze out all the milk this way. Then add another cup water to the coconut, and squeeze the milk out. Add the third cup water and mix, mash, and squeeze the liquid out into the cloth. Squeeze out the liquid from the cloth into the bowl. You will now have about 3½ cups of very lightly salted coconut milk.

5. To prepare coconut cream, pour the milk into a pan and bring to a boil over moderate heat. Reduce heat immediately to low and simmer slowly for about 20 minutes, or until a thickened white cream remains. Do not overcook or you will reduce everything to coconut oil.

Both the coconut milk and cream have their individual uses as indicated in the recipes.

HARD-COOKED EGGS, BURMESE STYLE

1. In a pan cover as many eggs as wanted with cold water. Bring to a boil over moderate heat and cook for 5 minutes.

2. Drain and run the eggs under cold water. Let them soak in the cold water for 5 minutes.

3. Cut the eggs into halves with a sharp knife or scissors *before peeling.* The yolk will still remain soft and semicooked. The egg is then scooped out of the shell and served or used as a garnish.

GARLIC OIL AND CRISPY GARLIC SLICES

8 medium-size garlic cloves
¼ cup corn or peanut oil

1. Cut the garlic cloves horizontally into thin slices.

2. Heat the oil in a wok, drop the garlic slices in, and fry over moderate heat for 2 to 3 minutes, until the slices turn light brown. Remove slices immediately from the oil and drain on paper towels.

3. Cool the oil. Place in a jar with a tight cover and refrigerate. Use as needed in salads or in cooking.

The garlic crisps may be made in any quantity. They can be stored in a jar with a tight cover to be used when needed.

MAKES 3 TABLESPOONS

MON-NYIN CHIN

Fermented Mustard Green Pickles

1 bunch of Chinese mustard greens, about 1½ pounds
3 carrots, sliced thin diagonally, about 3 cups
½ pound shallots, peeled
2 teaspoons dried hot red chili flakes
2 teaspoons salt
2 teaspoons brown sugar
½ teaspoon ground turmeric
1 cup beer

1. Rinse the mustard greens in water, leaf by leaf, to remove any sand. Soak the leaves in hot water for 15 minutes to wilt them. Drain well and cut into ¼-inch-wide slices.

2. Mix all the ingredients together in a bowl. Squeeze and press the vegetables together in a sort of kneading motion for 10 minutes. This will integrate the flavorings with the vegetables.

3. Cover the bowl and let the pickle ferment in a warm place or at room temperature for 3 days, then pack in covered jars. The pickle may be kept refrigerated for a month or more.

Serve at room temperature with any kind of Burmese food, but especially with Burmese-Style Fried Rice (see Index).

MAKES 1 PINT

CRISPY FRIED ONIONS

1 cup corn or peanut oil
⅛ teaspoon ground turmeric
1 pound small onions, sliced thin, about 2 cups
½ teaspoon sugar

1. Heat the oil in a skillet or wok over moderately low heat. Add the turmeric and onions. Fry slowly, stirring now and then, for 10 to 12 minutes, until the onions begin to turn color.

2. Add the sugar, stir well, and fry for about 2 minutes more. The onions should be light golden brown. Remove them and drain on paper towels.

Cool and store in a container with a tight cover. May be refrigerated for several weeks and used when needed.

Reserve the flavored oil under refrigeration and use for any kind of Burmese cooking or salad dressing.

MAKES 1 CUP

PEPYOAT

Cooked Garden Pea Sprouts

1 pound dried garden peas (known as vatana *in India)*

1. Cover the peas with water and soak for 8 to 10 hours, or over-night. The next day, drain well.

2. Line a colander with 2 wet paper towels. Put the peas into the colander and cover them with 2 more wet paper towels. Pour over the colander 2 cups water which, of course, will drain off. Cover the colander with a plate to eliminate light.

About 3 times daily pour 2 cups water over the colander to keep · the peas moist. Do this for 3 days. The peas will sprout. The sprouts are about 1 inch long.

3. Rinse the sprouted peas (which are the sprouts still attached to the peas) in water. Drain. Now put in an empty pan:

> *1 tablespoon corn or peanut oil*
> *the sprouted peas*
> *½ teaspoon baking soda*
> *1 teaspoon salt*
> *2 cups water*

4. Cover the pan, bring to a boil over moderately low heat, and cook for 30 minutes. Stir well, cover the pan, and cook for 20 minutes more so that the liquid has evaporated. Now the *pepyoat* is ready to be served at room temperature with rice. It may be used in various dishes, including Burmese-Style Fried Rice (see Index).

MAKES 2 CUPS

PEPOK

Fermented Soybeans

1 pound dried soybeans

1. Cover the soybeans with warm water and soak overnight. Drain the next day.

2. Cover the soybeans with fresh water and cook in a covered pan over moderate heat for 1½ hours, until the beans are soft but still retain their shape. Drain in a colander and cover immediately with aluminum foil.

3. Put the colander in a bowl and leave it in a warm place for the beans to ferment and produce a white fungus, which gradually appears.

During warm summer days the fermentation will take 3 to 4 days. Cooler seasons might take 1 week.

Pack the beans in jars, cover, and refrigerate for future use.

MAKES 1 PINT

APPETIZERS AND FRITTERS

The Burmese customs related to dining and entertaining differ from ours in many ways. They do not have large cocktail parties, or serve three or four separate courses at dinner. The food that we call "appetizers" they would serve when friends drop in for a visit between meals. With a cup of green tea and a fritter or a sweet (see Sweets chapter), the casual visit becomes a social occasion.

At mealtime, instead of many courses and large servings, the dining table is usually spread with numerous side dishes. This results in a variety of foods and flavors, but small portions of each. Many of the recipes in this chapter serve a double purpose: They may be used in your own home in small portions as appetizers, or in slightly larger ones as side dishes. Experiment!

KAW PYANT

Fresh Spring Roll

STUFFING

 1 tablespoon corn or peanut oil
 1 teaspoon brown sugar
 1 garlic clove, chopped fine
 2 cups fine-chopped cabbage
 2 cups coarse-chopped cauliflower
 2 cups bean sprouts, halved horizontally
 1 cup shredded carrot
 1 cup bamboo shoots (canned), shredded
 1 cup peeled and shredded rutabaga
 ¼ cup soy sauce
 ½ cup cellophane noodles, soaked in hot water for 10 minutes,
  drained, cut with scissors into 3-inch pieces

 1 package (10 skins) round Shanghai egg-roll skins (made of flour,
  water, salt)

GARNISHES

 Lettuce leaves, about 3 by 2 inches
 1 cup cooked roast pork (purchased in Chinese shop or
  homemade), chopped fine
 4 eggs, beaten, cooked into 5 thin omelets with a teaspoon of oil,
  folded over twice, cooled, chopped fine
 1 Chinese-style tofu, cut into 6 pieces, deep-fried in oil until brown
  all around, cooled, chopped fine
 ½ pound shrimps, cooked in the shell in boiling water for 5
  minutes, peeled, chopped fine
 2 scallions, green part only, sliced thin (or equal amount of
  Chinese chives)

1. Heat the oil in a wok and stir-fry the brown sugar and garlic for 5 seconds. Add the cabbage, cauliflower, bean sprouts, carrot, bamboo shoots, and rutabaga; stir-fry for 3 minutes as they wilt. Add the soy sauce and stir-fry for 2 minutes more. Add the cellophane noodles and stir a moment to mix. Set aside.

2. On each egg-roll skin put the garnishes in this order: 1 lettuce leaf on the skin, 1 heaping tablespoon stuffing on the end closest to you, then 2 teaspoons pork, 2 teaspoons chopped omelet, 2 teaspoons tofu; 2 teaspoons shrimp, 1 teaspoon scallion or chive over all.

3. Roll the skin over once, firmly. Fold over each side of the skin. Add 1 teaspoon of Sour Sauce Dip (see Index), then roll over and close the roll.

Serve at room temperature. Cut the roll into 4 equal pieces with scissors. Add additional sauce if wanted. Serve with scallion stems.

MAKES 8 TO 10 ROLLS

Variation: These rolls may also be deep-fried, in which case they are called *Kaw Pyant Kyaw,* Fried Spring Rolls. Prepare spring rolls as above but omit lettuce. Make a paste of 1 tablespoon flour and 2 tablespoons water and seal edges of spring rolls. Fry in deep fat for 3 or 4 minutes, or until brown. Serve warm with the Sour Sauce Dip.

HNIT PYAN KYAW

Twice-Fried Tohu

The *tohu* is a specialty of Taunggyi in the Shan State in Upper Burma. When twice fried, *tohu* has a crisp, brown exterior and a smooth, creamy interior, a remarkably tasty appetizer. I watched the lady vendor doing a brisk business in Taunggyi's marketplace, as she sliced and fried tohu for a crowd of buyers.

1. Cut as many pieces of *tohu* as you wish into 2-inch-long finger-thick slices.

2. Heat 1 cup of oil in a wok and over moderate heat fry the *tohu* pieces for about 3 minutes, or until they turn a golden color. Remove pieces from the oil and cool completely.

3. Return *tohu* to the oil and fry again until it is a crisp, light brown, about 3 minutes more. Drain on paper towels.

Serve as an appetizer.

ATHE AMYIT HIN

Chicken-Liver Appetizer

> 1 tablespoon corn or peanut oil
> 2 garlic cloves, chopped fine
> ⅛ teaspoon ground turmeric
> 1 teaspoon paprika
> ½ pound chicken gizzards, halved
> ½ pound chicken livers, divided into lobes
> 1 tablespoon fish sauce
> ½ teaspoon salt

1. Heat the oil in a skillet and fry the garlic, turmeric, and paprika over moderate heat for 1 minute. Add the gizzards and stir-fry for 2 minutes. Cover the pan and cook for 10 minutes.

2. Add the livers, fish sauce, and salt to taste. Stir a moment, cover the pan, and cook over moderately low heat for 5 minutes. Uncover and stir-fry for 2 minutes more to evaporate any liquid.

Serve warm as an appetizer. This may also be served as a garnish with Chicken Curry with Coconut Milk Gravy (On No Kyauk Swe, see Index.)

SERVES 6

PEBOK SI HLAW

Dry Roasted Soybeans

These beans make admirable nibbles with drinks. They are a specialty of the people of Inle Lake in the Shan State of Upper Burma.

> 1 pound soybeans
> 2 cups kosher salt

1. Rinse the beans well in room-temperature water and drain. Cover with fresh water and let them soak for 15 minutes. Drain in a sieve or colander and let the moist beans remain overnight in a container, covered with a kitchen towel.

2. Next day, heat the salt in a heavy metal skillet. Add the still moist soybeans and stir over moderately high heat for 10 to 15 minutes. The beans will become dry and crisp. Test the crispness by pinching a bean in your fingers. It should crack and crumble, indicating doneness.

3. Put through a metal sieve to sift out the salt. When beans are completely cool, store them in a jar with a tight cover.

The salt, which is now a grayish tan color, may be used in standard cooking.

MAKES 2 CUPS

MOGOK WETTHA KYAW
Crisp-Fried Pork Shreds

The crisp shreds are a specialty of Mogok, a town in Burma noted for its ruby mines, the finest in the world. There, the shreds are traditionally served as a side dish with a green mango salad or pickle and dhal (lentil) soup. They are fried in great quantities for parties or for the religious ceremonies involving the novitiate of young monks.

½ pound cooked pork shoulder, shredded into 1-inch-long pieces
1 teaspoon soy sauce
Oil for deep-frying

1. Mix the pork shreds and soy sauce together.

2. Heat the oil in a wok. With your fingertips pick up about 2 tablespoons of the shreds and gently drop them into the hot oil. Crisp-fry the small fritter that forms over moderate heat for 2 to 3 minutes. Remove and drain on paper towels.

Store the small fritters in a jar, or break them up into pieces.
Serve as an appetizer with drinks, or sprinkle generously over rice.

SERVES 6

GANAN TOFU

Crispy Cubed Tofu Surprise

This unusual and tasty appetizer, a modern Burmese dish, was created in Rangoon by a friend, U Maung Tin.

1 tablespoon salt
1 tablespoon sugar
½ teaspoon pepper
5 cups hot water
2 eggs, beaten
2½ cups cornmeal
½ cup flour
1 pound crabmeat
1 Chinese tofu cake, mashed with a fork
3 tablespoons corn or peanut oil
¼ cup cornstarch

1. Mix the salt, sugar, and pepper in 2 cups of the hot water. Add the eggs, cornmeal, and flour and mix well together.

2. Add the crabmeat and tofu to the mixture and stir well.

3. Put 2 tablespoons oil into a wok or large skillet and stir-fry the cornmeal mixture over moderate heat for 5 minutes. The mixture will become sticky.

4. Add the balance of water (3 cups) and continue to cook the mixture for 10 minutes more, to thicken.

5. Rub an aluminum foil or heatproof glass tray with 1 tablespoon oil. Pour in the mixture, which should come to a height of 1 inch, and smooth the surface. Place the tray into the freezing compartment of a refrigerator and freeze solid.

6. Remove the tray from freezer and cut the mixture into 1-inch cubes. Dust each cube with cornstarch and return them to the freezer.

7. When ready to use, remove as many pieces as wanted and deep-fry them in hot oil to a crisp brown. Drain well. Serve warm with a small dish of sugar and another of tomato ketchup.

SERVES 10

Variation: One pound of ground boneless chicken may be substituted for the crabmeat.

MARTHPE BAYAGYAW

Black Gram Puffs

The Indian name for black gram is *urd*, which is one of the dhal or so-called lentils used in soups all over India. The botanical name is *Phaseolus mungo*. The Burmese, typically, have given it their own treatment by combining it with plantain to make batter for these fried doughnuts, which they serve as appetizers.

2 cups dried black gram (urd dhal)
1 ripe plantain, with an almost black skin
1 teaspoon salt
¼ teaspoon ground turmeric
Oil for deep-frying, about 2 cups

1. Cover the black gram with water and soak for 5 hours. Drain well by first stirring rapidly to remove as many of the black skins as will come off. Drain through a metal sieve.

2. Process the gram with the plantain into a coarse paste. Mix in the salt and turmeric. Let the mixture stand, covered, in the refrigerator overnight.

3. Heat oil in a wok or skillet. Put 1 heaping tablespoon of the mixture into a saucer and flatten it out to 2½ inches in diameter and about ⅜ inch thick. Push your finger through the center and slide the "doughnut" into the hot oil. Brown on both sides over moderate heat for about 3 minutes. Drain on paper towels.

Serve at room temperature as a snack with tea, coffee, or drinks.

SERVES 8 TO 10

Note: A cookie press is a very effective implement for squeezing out the plantain batter to shape a round fritter with a center hole. This results in more uniform frying.

PEINU ASATHUT

Stuffed Taro-Root Cutlet

5 tablespoons corn or peanut oil
1 garlic clove, chopped
½ teaspoon chopped fresh ginger
1 small onion, chopped, ¼ cup
⅛ teaspoon ground turmeric
¾ teaspoon salt
¼ pound ground beef
1 pound taro
1 egg
⅛ teaspoon pepper

1. First make the stuffing: Heat 1 tablespoon of the oil in a skillet and fry the garlic, ginger, onion, turmeric, and ½ teaspoon of the salt over moderate heat for 2 minutes. Add the beef and stir-fry for about 3 minutes, or until the color changes. Put aside and cool.

2. Cook the taro root, not peeled, in enough water to cover for about 30 minutes, or until soft. Cool and peel. Cut the root into slices and process to a smooth purée or, as in the Burmese way, use a mortar and pestle.

3. Beat the egg, remaining ¼ teaspoon salt, and the pepper together.

4. Prepare the cutlets by dividing the taro purée into 6 equal parts. Flatten one part in the palm of your hand to make a circle 3 inches across and ½ inch thick.

5. Put 2 tablespoons of the stuffing in the center; fold the sides of the cutlet over the stuffing to make a mound. Flatten it out to a round disc 3 inches in diameter and ½ inch thick. Dip it into the beaten egg. Prepare all the cutlets in this way.

6. Heat the rest of the oil in a skillet and over moderate heat brown the cutlets for 5 minutes all around. Drain on paper towels.

Serve warm, as an appetizer or snack with tea or coffee.

MAKES 6 CUTLETS

Variations: One half cup of chopped raw shrimps is a fine substitute for the beef. Season the shrimps lightly with salt, pepper, and turmeric. Proceed as with beef stuffing.

Chopped lamb can also be used with the same flavoring as for the beef.

For vegetarians, prepare the cutlets without any stuffing. Dip them into the beaten egg and brown in the oil.

Mashed potato is a legitimate substitute for the taro root. Cook unpeeled potatoes and continue in the same manner as for taro.

MANDALAY PEGYAW

Red Kidney-Bean Fritters

1 cup dried red kidney beans
1 cup glutinous rice flour
½ cup water
1 teaspoon salt
1 teaspoon fine-chopped fresh ginger
1 teaspoon baking powder
Oil for deep-frying

1. Cover the beans with water and soak overnight.

2. Next day, drain well, then crush beans in a food processor to a coarse consistency.

3. Mix the rice flour, water, salt, ginger, and baking powder together. Add the beans and mix well. Set aside in a covered bowl for 1 hour.

4. Heat oil in a skillet. Prepare round fritters about 2 inches in diameter and ¼ inch thick. Brown them in the oil over moderate heat for 3 minutes. Drain on paper towels.

Serve warm.

MAKES 10 TO 12 FRITTERS

KALAPE KYAW

Split-Pea Fritters

These fritters, sometimes known as "bean toast," are usually served with the Classic Fish Soup, Mohinga. However, they are just as good served as appetizers with drinks or as a snack for the tea or coffee hour.

We used yellow split peas since they are easily available here in supermarkets. Traditionally, *channa ka dal* (lentils) are used, slightly smaller than the peas but with a flavor that would be difficult to differentiate from that of yellow split peas.

> *1 cup rice flour*
> *⅛ teaspoon ground turmeric*
> *3 cups dried yellow split peas, soaked in water overnight or for*
> *   about 12 hours, drained*
> *1½ cups water*
> *Oil for deep-frying*
> *Salt*

1. Mix everything together except oil and salt.

2. Heat oil in a skillet. Over moderate heat, pour in ¼ cup of the pea batter. Fry for 2 minutes, turn the fritter over, and brown it on the other side. The fritters will not be perfectly round.

3. When the fritter is brown, remove it with a slotted spoon and drain on paper towels. Remove any small bits of batter from the oil. Continue to fry all the fritters this way.

Serve warm or at room temperature, sprinkled with salt if you wish.

MAKES ABOUT 14 FRITTERS

PAYAGYAW

Spiced Yellow-Pea Fritter

The *payagyaw* is of Indian origin, introduced into Burma by immigrants. In Calcutta it is called the *piaju* (spelling is different but the pronunciation is about the same) and is made of almost the same ingredients but is shaped like a small pancake. Actually, the Burmese shape is more convenient to handle although a bit more trouble to make.

1 cup dried yellow split peas
1 medium-size onion, cut into thin slices, ½ cup
¼ cup chopped fresh coriander
1 fresh semihot green chili, chopped
½ teaspoon ground cuminseed
½ teaspoon salt
1 tablespoon Toasted Chick-Pea Flour (Besan, see Index)
½ teaspoon ground turmeric
¼ cup water
Oil for deep-frying

1. Cover the peas with water and soak overnight.

2. Next day, drain and process to a coarse consistency.

3. Mix the peas with onion, coriander, chili, cuminseed, salt, chick-pea flour, and turmeric. Add the ¼ cup water, mix well, and set aside for 1 hour.

4. Heat the oil in a wok or skillet. Prepare a ball with 1 heaping teaspoon of the pea mixture. Slightly flatten it and brown in the oil over moderate heat for about 2 minutes. Drain on paper towels.

Serve warm as an appetizer with drinks or a snack with tea or coffee.

MAKES 20 FRITTERS

KIN-BAUNG KYAW

Pork and Vegetable Fritters

This fine appetizer is a specialty from Taunggyi, the capital city of the Shan State in Upper Burma.

BATTER

> ½ cup standard rice flour
> 1 tablespoon glutinous rice flour
> ⅛ teaspoon salt
> ⅛ teaspoon ground turmeric
> 1 teaspoon soy sauce
> 1 teaspoon corn or peanut oil
> ½ cup cold water

MIXTURE

> 1 cup ¼-inch-cubes of boneless pork
> 1 teaspoon salt
> 1 teaspoon soy sauce
> ½ teaspoon sugar
> 1 cup ¼-inch-cubes of Chinese cabbage, white part only
> 1 cup ¼-inch-cubes of peeled chayote
> Oil for deep-frying

1. Mix the batter ingredients together until smooth.

2. Mix the pork, salt, soy sauce, and sugar together. Let stand for 15 minutes.

3. In a small round saucer, combine 1 heaping tablespoon each of the cabbage, chayote, pork, and batter. Mix well.

4. Heat oil in a skillet and slide the fritter mixture into the oil, keeping its round shape. Fry over moderate heat on both sides for about 4 minutes. Continue with the rest of the mixture. Drain on paper towels and serve with a dip.

Serve warm.

MAKES 8 TO 10 FRITTERS

KYETTHA TAUK TAUK KYAW

Chicken and Vegetable Fritters

1 cup chopped uncooked chicken
1 egg, beaten
½ teaspoon salt
½ cup grated carrot
½ cup grated white radish
½ cup grated cabbage
1 teaspoon fish sauce
½ teaspoon sugar (optional)
1 scallion, sliced thin
1 tablespoon chopped coriander
1 tablespoon chopped semihot green chili
1 tablespoon rice flour
¼ cup corn or peanut oil

1. Mix the chicken, egg, and salt together.

2. Add the carrot, radish, cabbage, fish sauce, sugar, scallion, coriander, and chili. Mix well. Add the rice flour and mix.

3. Heat the oil in a skillet. Prepare fritters 3 inches in diameter and ½ inch thick, using about ½ cup of mixture for each one. Brown them in the oil over moderate heat for about 2 minutes on each side. Drain on paper towels.

Serve warm as an appetizer or a side dish with any appropriate Burmese dip (see Index.)

MAKES 6 FRITTERS

PAZUN GWET KYAW

Shrimp and Bean-Sprout Fritter

¼ pound fresh bean sprouts, about 1 cup
½ pound small shrimps, peeled and deveined
1 Chinese tofu cake, cut into ½-inch cubes
1 cup Spicy Batter for Fried Vegetables (see Index)
Oil for deep-frying

1. Spread about 2 tablespoons bean sprouts in a small flat dish or saucer, about 3 inches in diameter. Place 1 shrimp on each side, and put 2 tofu cubes in the center of this arrangement. Dribble 1 heaping tablespoon of the batter over all and let it seep down to hold the fritter together.

2. Heat oil in a wok or skillet. Slide the fritter into the oil without disturbing its shape. Brown on both sides over moderate heat for about 3 minutes. Drain on paper towels.

Serve warm as an appetizer with any appropriate Burmese dip.

MAKES 2 FRITTERS

Note: The small dish or saucer helps in preparing a round fritter, and in sliding it easily into the oil. Otherwise, one could mix the ingredients with the fritter batter and drop them into the hot oil, a heaping tablespoon at a time. Somehow the Burmese system makes this more interesting.

PAZUN KYAW

Shrimp Puff

½ pound medium shrimps, peeled and deveined, cut into ½-inch
  pieces
⅔ cup thin-sliced celery, leaves and young stems
1 Chinese tofu cake, cut into ½-inch cubes
¼ teaspoon ground turmeric
¼ teaspoon salt
½ cup Spicy Batter for Fried Vegetables (see Index)
Oil for deep-frying

1. Combine the shrimps, celery, tofu, turmeric, salt, and batter.
Mix well.

2. For each puff, put about 2 tablespoons of the mixture into a
saucer.

3. Heat oil in a wok or skillet. Slide mixture from the saucer into
the oil without disturbing its shape. Brown on both sides over moderate
heat for 3 minutes. Drain on paper towels.

Serve warm with any Burmese dip.

MAKES 6 TO 8 PUFFS

Note: Shaping the round fritter by putting it into a small round
dish is the traditional and practical Burmese method. Of course, one
could simply scoop out a heaping tablespoon of the mixture and fry
the puffs that way.

AKYAW SON

Assorted Fried Vegetables in Batter

This is a great appetizer—a preparation in which a large assortment of vegetables, meat, and fritters can be prepared a short time before serving and lightly reheated in a 400°F. oven. Of course, with some kitchen assistance, the fritters may be fried and served immediately.

1 cup corn or peanut oil for deep-frying
1 recipe Spicy Batter for Fried Vegetables (see Index)
Calabash, not peeled, cut into finger shapes
Chayote, finger-size sticks, ½ inch thick
Small eggplant, cut into ¼-inch-thick slices
Banana, quartered (if small sugar bananas, cook whole)
Onions, sliced

Heat the oil in a wok. Dip assorted pieces of the vegetables, one at a time, into the batter, and fry until golden. Drain on paper towels and serve immediately. Note that the onion rings should be dipped into the batter 4 or 5 rings together and made into a rough circle of overlapping onion rings. Transfer them to the fat with a spatula.

Serve with the Achin (Sour Sauce Dip, see Index) or any other dip of your choice.

Variations: Add very small fresh shrimps in shells. Mix shrimps with the batter and use 1 heaping tablespoon of the mixture to make fritters about 3 inches in diameter.

Fish fillet, cut into ¼-inch dice. Mix with the batter and prepare 3-inch fritters as for the shrimps.

Boneless pork, sliced thin into 1-inch pieces. Dip into batter and fry until golden brown on both sides.

Boneless chicken breast, cut into 2-inch-long strips, ¼ inch thick. Dip into batter and fry until golden brown.

Chopped onions, added to the batter. Prepare 3-inch fritters with the mixture. Brown on both sides.

CHUTNEYS AND CONDIMENTS

PONYEE GYI THOAT

Fermented Black-Bean Paste Chutney

¼ cup Fermented Black-Bean Paste (Pagan Ponyee Gyi, see
    Index)
1 garlic clove, chopped fine
1 tablespoon shrimp powder
¼ teaspoon salt
2 tablespoons corn or peanut oil
1 teaspoon dried hot red chili flakes (optional)

Mix everything together smoothly.

Serve at room temperature with rice, or on bread as an appetizer
or luncheon snack. Include the chili if you wish a spicier chutney.

MAKES ⅓ CUP

PEDI CHIN

Fermented Bean Sprouts

Although this is primarily a condiment, the fermented bean sprouts are also served as a salad. Sprinkle with toasted sesame seeds, sliced onions that have been rinsed under cold water and dried, and Crispy Fried Onions (see Index). Season with a teaspoon or two of the oil in which the onions have been fried.

This is a country salad. It is served at village celebrations with a pork dish and Hot and Sour Dried Shrimp Garnish (Balachong No. 1, see Index).

1 cup uncooked rice
3 cups water
2 teaspoons salt
Pinch of ground turmeric
1 pound fresh bean sprouts

1. Rinse the rice with the 3 cups water. Pour off and reserve the water. (Use the rice for another purpose.)

2. Mix the rice water with salt and turmeric. 'Pour this over the bean sprouts in a glass jar with a tight cover. Allow the sprouts to ferment at room temperature for 3 days. Refrigerate afterwards.

Serve as a pickle with Burmese or Western foods as you wish.

MAKES ABOUT 6 CUPS

THAYET THI ACHO THANAT

Green Mango Chutney

1 large green unripe mango, 1 pound
¼ cup sugar, more or less
½ teaspoon salt
¼ cup cider or white vinegar

1. Do not peel the mango. Cut it into thin, long strips including the skin. Discard the seed.

2. Mix all the ingredients together in a pan. Cook over moderately low heat, covered, for 10 minutes.

3. Uncover and stir continuously for about 10 minutes more. The liquid should be evaporated and the mango softened.

Serve at room temperature, or chilled, with pork dishes or any Burmese curries. The chutney will keep for 2 weeks if refrigerated.

MAKES 1½ CUPS

THAYET YO

Ripe Mango Chutney

2 large ripe mangoes, about 2 pounds
3 tablespoons cider or white vinegar
½ teaspoon salt
1 to 2 tablespoons sugar
1 teaspoon fresh ginger juice (Crush 1 inch of fresh ginger in a
*   mortar, which will release the juice.)*
2 teaspoons lemon or lime juice

1. Peel the ripe mangoes and cut into thin slices.

2. Put everything into a pan and cook over moderately low heat for 15 to 20 minutes. This will reduce the mango to an applesauce consistency.

Serve at room temperature, or chilled, with pork or other meat dishes. Can be kept for 2 weeks under refrigeration.

MAKES 1 PINT

KHAYAN CHIN THI NGAPI CHET

Tomato Chutney

This is a fine homemade chutney, which can be served with vegetarian, fish, or meat dishes. It has enough flavor and substance to provide authority to plain boiled rice.

2 tablespoons corn or peanut oil
¼ teaspoon ground turmeric
½ teaspoon paprika
1 small onion, sliced, ¼ cup
1 garlic clove, sliced
1 tablespoon shrimp powder
1 teaspoon shrimp paste
1 tablespoon fish sauce
2 tablespoons water
1 large ripe tomato, fresh or canned, peeled and cut into 1-inch
    pieces, about 1 cup
1 hot green chili, stem and seeds removed, cut into thin slices
1 scallion, cut into ½-inch pieces
1 tablespoon chopped fresh coriander

1. Heat the oil in a skillet, add the turmeric, paprika, onion, and garlic, and stir-fry over moderate heat until onion is golden. Add the shrimp powder and shrimp paste and stir-fry for 2 minutes.

2. Add the fish sauce, water, and tomato. Stir-fry for 5 minutes.

3. Add the chili, scallion, and coriander. Mix well.

Serve at room temperature with any Burmese food.

MAKES ½ CUP

THAMBAYA THI THANAT
Lime Pickle

This pickle should be made in the summertime when limes are easily available and the sun shines frequently. This is a luscious pickle, tart but with a suggestion of sweetness. The trick is to pickle the limes in the salt for at least a month to allow limes to "ripen," and only then combine with the other ingredients.

4 green limes, quartered
2 teaspoons salt
2 tablespoons corn or peanut oil
1 inch of fresh ginger, cut into 4 slices
1 tablespoon white or cider vinegar
2 tablespoons sugar
1 tablespoon paprika
1 teaspoon garam masala
1 teaspoon ground cuminseed
2 garlic cloves, sliced

1. Squeeze out about half of the juice from the lime quarters and reserve it for another purpose. Mix 1 teaspoon salt with the lime pieces and put them in a jar with a tight cover. Leave in a sunny window for 4 days.

2. Mix remaining teaspoon of salt with the limes and let them pickle in the jar for at least 1 month. (Some say 2 months.)

3. After that, heat the oil in a skillet, add the ginger, and fry over moderately low heat for 1 minute, or until ginger is lightly browned.

4. Add the vinegar, the limes and the liquid that has accumulated in the jar, and the sugar. Mix well and continue cooking until the vinegar has evaporated. Add the paprika, *garam masala*, cuminseed, and garlic. Stir-fry for 3 minutes.

5. Cool the mixture and store in a jar with a tight cover. The pickle may be left out on a kitchen shelf or refrigerated.

Serve with any kind of Burmese or Indian dish.

MAKES 1 PINT

THAYET THI THANAT

Mango Pickle, Sweet and Sour

8 garlic cloves, peeled, about ¼ cup
1 cup white or cider vinegar
1 cup corn or peanut oil
2 teaspoons fine-sliced fresh ginger
½ pound dried mango, 3 cups loosely measured (see Note)
½ cup sugar
2 tablespoons paprika
2 teaspoons garam masala
2 teaspoons ground cuminseed

1. Soak the garlic in the vinegar overnight. Remove garlic and set aside.

2. Heat the oil in a pan or skillet, add the ginger, fry over moderate heat for a few seconds, and remove the pan to cool.

3. Put the vinegar, mango, and sugar in another pan and cook over moderate heat, covered, for 5 minutes, which softens the mango considerably. Remove pan from heat.

4. Add the soaked garlic, the paprika, *garam masala*, and cuminseed to the mango pan and stir well. Finally, add the oil and ginger and mix thoroughly. (The oil and vinegar are both preservatives and are drained out when serving the pickle.)

5. Cool. Store the pickle in a jar with a tight cover. It may be kept on the kitchen shelf or in the refrigerator indefinitely.

Serve the pickle with any kind of Burmese or Indian food, but it is especially good with lamb, beef, and vegetarian dishes.

MAKES 1 PINT

Note: Dried mango may be purchased in Indian food shops. However, it is recommended that you prepare your own in this relatively simple way: During the mango season, purchase 1 or 2 large, green, firm mangoes. Cut long strips of fruit from the seed out, including the skin, and cut these into 2-inch-square pieces. Lay the pieces out in a sunny window for 3 days to dry partly. Then proceed with the recipe.

NGAPI CHET

Anchovy Dip

In Burma this dip is used as a chutney or table condiment with mild-flavored meat or vegetables, and it is a potent and popular addition to any meal. As a dip, it is best served with a selection of raw vegetables.

1 bottle or can (3 to 4 ounces) anchovy fillets
1 garlic clove, chopped
1 tablespoon sliced onion
⅛ teaspoon ground turmeric
¼ teaspoon paprika
1 semihot red or green chili, seeded, sliced
1 large ripe tomato, peeled, seeded, cut into 1-inch cubes
2 scallions, sliced

1. Using the anchovy oil from the can, fry the garlic, onion, turmeric, and paprika in a skillet over moderate heat for 2 minutes.

2. Add the anchovy fillets, chili, and tomato and stir-fry for 3 minutes. Add the scallion and stir for 1 minute.

Serve at room temperature.

SERVES 6

NGA YOK CHIN
Red Chili Dip

2 tablespoons small hot red chili, fresh or pickled in vinegar, sliced
    thin
2 garlic cloves, crushed in a mortar
1 tablespoon chopped fresh coriander
Juice of 1 whole fresh lime
2 teaspoons sugar
1 teaspoon fish sauce
½ teaspoon salt
2 teaspoons soy sauce

Mix everything together.

Serve as a dip at room temperature, especially with crispy fried Pork Roll (Wettha Leik, see Index).

SERVES 6

ACHIN
Sour Sauce Dip

2 garlic cloves, sliced
½ inch of fresh ginger, sliced
2 tablespoons tamarind paste, soaked in 1 cup water, strained
1 tablespoon honey
1 teaspoon sugar
1 tablespoon soy sauce
2 teaspoons fish sauce
½ teaspoon salt
1 teaspoon paprika
½ teaspoon dried hot red chili flakes

Crush the garlic and ginger in a processor. Add all other ingredients and process to a smooth sauce.

Serve with any type of Burmese food but especially with Assorted Fried Vegetables in Batter (Akyaw Son, see Index).

MAKES ¼ CUP

BALACHONG # 1

Hot and Sour Dried Shrimp Garnish

This recipe for *balachong* has a smoother texture than the one for *balachong # 2* and has the assertive flavor given by the acid pulp of the tamarind paste. This is so good and rich with flavor that it may be served as an appetizer on good bread or toast. Add more chili if you like, but 2 teaspoons is sufficient to stimulate most taste buds without overdoing it.

   1 tablespoon shrimp paste
   1 tablespoon tamarind paste, dissolved in 2 tablespoons water,
      strained
   2 tablespoons corn or peanut oil
   1 teaspoon paprika
   1 to 2 teaspoons hot red chili flakes
   ⅛ teaspoon ground turmeric
   ½ cup shrimp powder
   ½ cup Crispy Fried Onions (see Index)
   2 tablespoons Crispy Garlic Slices (see Index)

1. Mix the shrimp paste and tamarind liquid together.

2. Heat the oil in a skillet. Add the paprika, hot chili flakes, and turmeric and stir-fry over moderate heat for a moment.

3. Add the shrimp powder and mix well for 1 minute. Add the shrimp paste/tamarind mixture and stir-fry for 1 minute more.

4. Lastly, add the onion and garlic crisps. Stir quickly to mix and remove from the heat.

Serve at room temperature.

MAKES 1 CUP

BALACHONG # 2

Dried Crisp Shrimp Garnish

1 cup dried shrimps, 4 ounces
¼ cup peanut or corn oil
1 tablespoon dried hot red chili flakes, or more
1 cup Crispy Fried Onions (see Index)
1 tablespoon cider vinegar
¼ cup Crispy Garlic Slices (see Index)

1. Put the shrimps in a processor and cut them into coarse bits.

2. Heat the oil in a wok or skillet, add the shrimps and chili flakes, and stir-fry over moderate heat for 1 minute.

3. Add the onions, vinegar, and garlic and stir-fry for 2 minutes more. The mixture should be dry.

Serve at room temperature as a garnish for rice, curries, and vegetables.

MAKES 2 CUPS

Note: *Balachong* is probably the most popular condiment in Burma. It should be stored in a jar with a tight cover. Although it does not have to be refrigerated, if you store the jar in a freezer it will keep indefinitely.

SEIN-SA NGAPI CHET

Shrimp and Shrimp Paste Dip

2 teaspoons corn or peanut oil
⅛ teaspoon ground turmeric
1 tablespoon sliced onion
1 garlic clove, chopped fine
1 teaspoon fresh ginger, chopped fine
½ cup small shrimps, peeled and deveined
1 semihot chili, sliced, seeds removed
1 tablespoon shrimp paste, dissolved in 2 tablespoons water
1 teaspoon tamarind paste, dissolved in 2 tablespoons water,
    strained

1. Heat the oil in a wok and fry the turmeric, onion, garlic, and ginger until light brown, about 2 minutes. Add the shrimps and stir-fry for 1 minute, then add the chili and stir-fry for 1 minute more.

2. Add the shrimp paste liquid and tamarind liquid and stir-fry for 2 minutes as the liquids boil.

Serve at room temperature.

MAKES ¾ CUP

Note: This dip is a table condiment popular in some villages at the delta of the famous Irrawaddy River. In Burma, they would use 6 to 8 of the tiny, but dynamic, "bud eye" chilies in this native dish, as if in a contest to prove who could eat the hottest food. We have cut down on the amount in this version, so if you like your food really hot, experiment by using more chili.

NGAPI PHOKE

Baked Shrimp Paste

There is a Burmese proverb that admonishes, "If the teacher doesn't instruct properly, the pupil will fail, no matter how easy the task." So here are complete instructions for a very easy recipe.

2 tablespoons bottled shrimp paste
1 tablespoon thin-sliced semihot chili
2 tablespoons lime juice

1. Put the shrimp paste in a dish and shape into a small round cake about 3 inches in diameter and ¼ inch thick. Push your finger into the cake to make 8 depressions. Bake in a hot oven (400° F.) for about 5 minutes, so that a light crust forms on top.

2. Remove from the oven and mash the paste. Add the chili and lime juice and mix well.

Serve this condiment at room temperature with any type of Burmese curried dishes as well as with rice dishes. This is a powerful condiment, to be used in moderation.

SOUPS

It is an anomaly, upon reflection, to consider having soup in a humid, hot tropical climate such as Burma's. No matter what the temperature may be, soup is the beverage that accompanies the food. One dines on both simultaneously. There is a small but vital qualification—soup is served at room temperature, not piping hot. Considering that the temperature might be 90 degrees, this seems logical. I am referring here only to the light clear soups of daily dining such as Clear Shrimp and Lime Soup (Pazun Hin Cho, see Index).

There are also complex, vividly seasoned soups of fish or meat and a number of other ingredients (see Classic Fish Soup, Mohinga), which are remarkable concoctions and could be considered a one-dish meal. Here, no timid seasonings are found since shrimp paste, fish sauce, paprika, onion, ginger, garlic, chili, and tamarind are assertive and compelling.

Burmese soups are satisfying no matter what their composition, simple or complex, and regardless of hot, dry summers or monsoon torrents.

PENILAY HINCHO

Red Lentil Soup

This is a standard lentil soup, so easily assembled and so traditional, that it is almost automatically kept on the table during an entire Burmese meal.

½ cup dried red lentils
2 tablespoons corn or peanut oil
2 garlic cloves, chopped fine
½ inch of fresh ginger, chopped fine
¼ teaspoon ground turmeric
4 cups water
½ teaspoon salt, or more

1. Rinse the lentils well in cold water. Remove any small stones and lentil husks. Cover with cold water and soak for 1 hour. Drain well.

2. Heat the oil in a pan, add the garlic, ginger, and turmeric, and stir-fry over moderate heat for 1 minute. Add the lentils and brown them in the oil for 2 minutes.

3. Add the 4 cups water and cook for about 30 minutes, or until lentils are soft. Add the salt, and stir.

Serve hot.

SERVES 4

PEGYI HIN

Peeled Lima Bean Soup

In the springtime, when the *coccina* leaves (acacia family) are available in the countryside, the Burmese pick them to garnish this fine light soup. It is therefore considered a traditional spring soup. I have substituted watercress as being the commonest green with a flavor reminiscent of *coccina*.

1 cup peeled lima beans (see Note)
⅛ teaspoon ground turmeric
1 tablespoon corn or peanut oil
3 cups water
1 small onion, sliced thin, ¼ cup
1 teaspoon salt
1 tablespoon fish sauce
½ bunch of watercress, leaves and young stems

1. Put the lima beans, turmeric, and oil in a pan and stir-fry over moderate heat for 5 minutes.

2. Add the water, bring to a boil, and cook in a covered pan until lima beans are soft, about 30 minutes. Add the onion, salt, and fish sauce and cook for 5 minutes more.

3. Put several watercress sprigs in individual serving bowls and pour in the soup.

Serve warm.

SERVES 6

Note: To peel lima beans, cover them with water and soak them overnight. The next day, take the beans out, one at a time, and lightly squeeze them. The inner bean halves will pop out. Discard the skins. The Burmese are so fastidious they will not eat the coarse skins of the beans, but I sometimes do not bother with this step.

BUTHI HINCHO

Soup with Bottle Gourd

Buthi hincho is a classic soup served as an accompaniment to the meal. You will notice that the names of simple soups such as this one always end in *-cho*, whereas a more complex soup would have a name ending in *-ga.*

6 *cups water*
1 *tablespoon dried shrimp powder*
¼ *cup onion slices*
1 *garlic clove, pounded in a mortar*
1 *teaspoon shrimp paste*
1 *tablespoon fish sauce*
1 *teaspoon salt, or more*
1 *cup pieces of bottle gourd, 1 inch long and ¼ inch thick*

1. Put everything except the bottle gourd into a pan. Simmer the soup over low heat for 15 minutes.

2. Add the gourd and cook for 10 minutes more, which is sufficient time to soften but not overcook the gourd.

Serve warm throughout a Burmese meal.

SERVES 4

Variation: To alter the soup somewhat and make it spicier, pound together 2 garlic cloves and ¼ teaspoon ground pepper. Add this to the soup and let it simmer the entire length of time. When this is done the soup is known as *buthi hinga.*

BE BAUNG KYAM SAING

Shredded Duck Soup-Stew

This is a Sino-Burmese recipe that has been thoroughly Burmanized by adding ingredients that give it more flavor. It can be served as a soup with rice on the side, or it can be cooked for another 5 minutes and served as a main-dish stew.

DUCK

> *1 pound duck legs or breast, skinned*
> *1 inch of fresh ginger, cracked*
> *2 tablespoons soy sauce*
> *8 cups water*

SOUP

> *1 tablespoon corn or peanut oil*
> *2 garlic cloves, chopped fine*
> *½ inch of fresh ginger, chopped fine*
> *1 small onion, sliced, ¼ cup*
> *3 cups Fermented Mustard Green Pickles (Mon-Nyin Chin, see Index)*
> *2 teaspoons soy sauce*
> *2 eggs, beaten*
> *2 cups celery leaves, chopped coarse*

1. Cook the duck with the cracked ginger, soy sauce, and 8 cups water in a covered pan over moderate heat for 45 minutes, or until the duck is tender. Remove the duck, cool, and shred it. Reserve the broth but skim off the fat.

2. Heat the corn oil in a pan and stir-fry the garlic, chopped ginger, and onion slices over moderate heat for 3 minutes. Add the shredded duck meat and stir-fry for 2 minutes.

3. Add the mustard greens and soy sauce and stir-fry for a moment. Add the eggs and mix together slowly until the eggs set.

4. Add the reserved duck broth, bring to a boil, and simmer for 5 minutes. Add the celery leaves and stir a minute to blend flavors.

Serve warm with rice and other dishes.

SERVES 8

KYAZAN CHET

Noodles, Cloud Ear, and Golden Needle Soup

This is an extraordinarily rich family-style soup, which can be prepared for any size group by multiplying or dividing all ingredients. It is kept for special occasions since some of the ingredients (such as cloud ears) are expensive. Boneless chicken and the dried soybean (*yuba*) are both rich in protein, and the fresh garnishes add piquancy to an already savory combination.

> ½ *pound cellophane noodles*
> 2 *ounces (½ package) dried cloud ears*
> 2 *ounces dried day lily buds (golden needles)*
> 2 *lengths of dried soybean (yuba)*
> ¼ *cup corn or peanut oil*
> 1 *medium-size onion, chopped, about ½ cup*
> 2 *garlic cloves, chopped*
> 1 *inch of fresh ginger, chopped*
> ⅛ *teaspoon ground turmeric*
> 2 *teaspoons paprika*
> 1 *pound boneless uncooked chicken, both white and dark meat, cut*
>   *into ½-inch cubes*
> 20 *cups homemade chicken broth*
> 1 *teaspoon salt*
> ¼ *cup fish sauce*
> ½ *teaspoon ground pepper*

GARNISHES
> 1 *cup sliced scallions, green part only*
> ½ *cup chopped fresh coriander*
> *Lime slices*
> *Dried hot red chili flakes, toasted lightly in dry skillet*

1. Soak the noodles in hot water for 20 minutes. Drain well and cut into 4-inch pieces with scissors. Set aside.

2. Soak the cloud ears in hot water for 20 minutes. Rinse well to remove bits of sand. The cloud ears expand several times their size when soaked. Cut them into 2- or 3-inch strips, ½ inch wide.

3. Soak the lily buds in hot water for 10 minutes. Drain. Tie each bud into a knot so that it will have a firmer texture and will not fall apart in the soup.

4. Soak the dried soybean in hot water for 10 minutes, then cut it into ½-inch pieces with scissors. Set aside.

5. Heat the oil in a large pan and over moderate heat stir-fry the onion, garlic, ginger, turmeric, and paprika until light brown. Add the chicken pieces and stir-fry for 10 minutes.

6. Add the broth and bring to a boil. Add the cellophane noodles, cloud ears, day lilies, and soybean *(yuba)*. Add the salt, fish sauce, and pepper. Cook for 10 minutes more to integrate the flavors.

Serve hot, sprinkled with the garnishes and as much lime as wanted.

SERVES 10 TO 12

KYAUK-PHA-YON-THI HINCHO

Winter Melon Soup

4 cups water
1 garlic clove, cracked
2 shallots, peeled and quartered
4 fresh medium shrimps, peeled and deveined
2 teaspoons fish sauce
½ teaspoon salt
1 pound winter melon, peeled, seeds and soft pulp discarded, cut
    into ¼-inch-thick slices

1. Bring the water to a boil in a pan. Add the garlic, shallots, shrimps, fish sauce, and salt. Cook over moderate heat for 5 minutes.

2. Add the winter melon slices, cover the pan, and cook for 10 minutes, or until melon is soft and translucent. Adjust the seasoning and add more fish sauce if you desire.

Serve hot.

SERVES 4

SET HNIT MYO HINCHO

Dozen Ingredients Soup

This is a great many-faceted soup. It would be ideal in the American kitchen on cold winter days, served family-style.

BROTH

> ½ chicken, about 1¾ pounds, loose skin discarded
> ½ pound chicken gizzards
> 10 cups water
> 3 tablespoons fish sauce
> ½ teaspoon salt
> ½ inch of fresh ginger, cracked
> 1 garlic clove, cracked

VEGETABLES

> 1 tablespoon corn or peanut oil
> ½ cup thin-sliced onion
> ½ inch of fresh ginger, sliced thin
> 2 garlic cloves, sliced thin
> 2 teaspoons shrimp sauce
> ½ pound cauliflower, cut into thin 1-inch pieces
> 3 cups ½-inch-wide cabbage strips
> ½ cup dried mushrooms, soaked in water for 1 hour, drained, cut
>   into halves
> 1 cup dried day lily buds, soaked in water for 30 minutes, drained,
>   tied into knots
> 1 length of dried soybean (yuba), soaked in water for 30 minutes,
>   drained, cut into 1-inch pieces
> 1 medium-size zucchini, cut into ¼-inch slices
> 1 Chinese tofu cake, cut into 1-inch cubes
> 2 eggs, beaten
> 2 scallions, cut into slices
> 1 cup ½-inch pieces of young celery ribs and leaves
> ½ teaspoon black pepper (optional)

1. Put all the ingredients for the broth together in a pan. Bring to a boil, cover the pan, and cook over moderate heat for 30 minutes.

2. Remove chicken and gizzards. Cut the meat from the bones in long slender pieces. Cut the gizzards into ½-inch slices. Return the bones to the broth and simmer over moderately low heat for 30 minutes or more. Strain.

3. Heat the oil for the vegetables in a large pan and stir-fry the onion, ginger, and garlic over moderate heat for 3 minutes, or until golden. Add the chicken meat and gizzards and stir-fry for 1 minute more. Stir in the shrimp sauce.

4. Add the soup broth, bring to a boil, and add the cauliflower. As it continues cooking, add the cabbage and mushrooms, the day lily buds and dried soybean (*yuba*). Cook and stir for 2 minutes.

5. Add the zucchini and tofu. Cook for 2 minutes. When the soup returns to the boil, stir in the eggs.

6. Finally, add scallions and celery. Stir for a moment or two until hot and well blended.

Serve the soup hot, in the pan, family style. Sprinkle with pepper if you wish.

SERVES 10

Variation: For those who wish to enrich the soup even more, add ½ pound small shrimps, peeled and deveined. Add these after the tofu and before stirring in the eggs.

TATAPAW

Karen Special Soup

The Karens are a Burmese native tribe who live in Lower Burma on the border of Thailand. This soup, a specialty of theirs, has an interesting and imaginative flavor because of the toasted rice.

¾ cup uncooked rice
10 cups water
½ pound boneless pork, cut into ½-inch cubes
1 can (8 ounces) sliced bamboo shoots, drained
1 teaspoon salt
1 teaspoon shrimp paste
2 tablespoons shrimp sauce
1 inch of fresh ginger, crushed to a paste
3 garlic cloves, crushed to a paste
1 medium-size onion, chopped, ½ cup
½ teaspoon ground turmeric
½ teaspoon paprika
¼ teaspoon black pepper

1. Toast the rice in a dry skillet over moderately low heat until it becomes light brown. Break up the rice coarsely in a processor.

2. Bring the water to a boil in a large pan. Add the rice, pork, and all other ingredients. Cook over moderate heat for 30 minutes.

Serve hot as a soup. It also may be eaten as a sauce by pouring it over plain rice.

SERVES 8

KYAZAN PYOAT

Pork and Noodle Soup

The Burmese have a saying: "The best meat is pork, the best leaf is tea, the best fruit is mango." This pork and noodle soup is just one of the recipes that shows their practice of using up every part of the animal. It is a big-town, rather than country-style, mixed soup and is also known as *kye-o* or "copper pot" soup. It was probably a Chinese soup adapted to suit Burmese taste.

½ pound ground pork
1 teaspoon cornstarch
1 teaspoon soy sauce
1 teaspoon white or brown sugar
¼ teaspoon toasted sesame oil
½ teaspoon salt
6 cups pork broth or water
½ cup pork liver, cut into slices 2 inches long, ¼ inch thick
½ pork kidney, trimmed of fat and veins, cut into slices 2 inches long, ¼ inch thick
½ pound thin rice noodles, soaked in boiling water for 5 minutes, drained
2 tablespoons chopped celery leaves and ribs

1. Prepare meatballs by mixing together the pork, cornstarch, soy sauce, sugar, sesame oil, and salt. Shape balls ¾ inch in diameter. Set aside.

2. Bring the pork broth or water to a boil over moderate heat. Add the meatballs and simmer for 5 minutes. Add the liver and kidney slices and the noodles. Cover the pan and cook for 5 minutes more.

Serve the soup hot, sprinkled with the celery.

SERVES 6

U PONNYA'S NWA MEE HINGA

Grilled Oxtail and Watercress Soup

U Ponnya, a celebrated Burmese poet born in 1813, was a favorite in the king's court at Mandalay. Due to some confusion or political error, he was executed by mistake in 1868, but his writings are known to this day. In one of his poems he described "How to use the whole ox," from horn to hoof, and this century-old recipe for oxtail soup is named after him. The combination of oxtail and watercress gives the soup a rather unconventional flavor and makes it a fine luncheon dish. It is reputed to be nourishing for nursing mothers. Watercress is our substitute for the traditional green known as "chaste leaf" or "Indian wild pepper" (*Vitex trifolia*), *kyaung-ban* in Burmese.

1 pound oxtail, divided into sections
2 garlic cloves, chopped fine
1 tablespoon fish sauce
½ teaspoon salt
4 cups water
⅛ teaspoon pepper
½ bunch of watercress, divided into stems

1. Broil the oxtail in a gas or electric broiler until well roasted and slightly charred, about 15 minutes. Better still, barbecue over charcoal to impart a slightly smoky flavor.

2. Put everything except the watercress into a pan, and bring to a boil. Cover the pan and cook over moderately low heat for 1 hour or more to tenderize the meat until it comes away from the bone.

3. Add the watercress, cover the pan, and cook for 3 minutes more.

Serve hot.

SERVES 4

MONLA OU CHINYE

Japanese Radish in Tamarind Soup

This is a basic sour fish soup, which can be altered according to the vegetables used. Substitutes for the radish are chayote and zucchini. The Burmese also enjoy strips of green papaya in place of the radish.

½ pound porgy, red snapper, or similar fish, cut into 3 pieces
2 teaspoons shrimp paste
1 tablespoon fish sauce
¼ teaspoon salt
¼ teaspoon ground turmeric
1 teaspoon paprika
1 tablespoon corn or peanut oil
½ cup fine-chopped onion
1 garlic clove, chopped fine
1 teaspoon fine-chopped fresh ginger
1 small tomato, chopped
2 pounds white Japanese radish, peeled, cut into finger-size pieces
1 tablespoon tamarind paste, dissolved in 1 cup water, strained
6 cups water
1 tablespoon chopped fresh coriander

1. Put all ingredients into a pan except the tamarind, water, and coriander. Mix well.

2. Cook the mixture over moderate heat until the radish is tender, about 10 minutes.

3. Add the tamarind liquid and the water. Bring to a boil and simmer, covered, over moderately low heat for 20 minutes.

Serve warm sprinkled with coriander.

SERVES 6

BUDHI CHEN YE

Sour and Hot Fish and Calabash Soup

1 garlic clove, sliced
¼ inch of fresh ginger, sliced
1 small onion, sliced, ¼ cup
½ pound fish with bone—red snapper, porgy, or sea bass—cut into
    ½-inch-wide slices
2 cups half-moon slices of peeled calabash
1 tablespoon fish sauce
¾ teaspoon shrimp paste
½ teaspoon salt
1 tablespoon corn or peanut oil
½ teaspoon dried hot red chili flakes
¼ teaspoon ground turmeric
½ teaspoon paprika
2 tablespoons tamarind paste, soaked in 1 cup water for 15
    minutes, then strained
½ cup water
1 tablespoon fresh coriander leaves

1. Crush the garlic, ginger, and onion together in a processor to make a smooth paste. Put this in a large saucepan with the fish, calabash, fish sauce, shrimp paste, salt, oil, chili flakes, turmeric, and paprika. Stir this mixture over moderately low heat for 3 minutes.

2. Cover the pan and cook until the calabash becomes soft, about 5 minutes more.

3. Add the tamarind liquid and the ½ cup water, bring to a boil, and simmer over low heat for 5 minutes. Add the coriander and simmer for 2 minutes more.

Serve hot.

SERVES 4

Variations: Japanese radish, peeled and cut into finger-size pieces, is one substitute for the calabash. Chayote, peeled and sliced, is another.

SAN HLAW HIN

Toasted Rice and Fish Soup

This soup has much to recommend it. The classic Burmese flavorings (lemongrass, turmeric, ginger) give it tang, and the toasted rice provides an unusual texture.

*½ pound whole fish—porgy, sea bass, red snapper—cut into
    1-inch-wide slices
¼ teaspoon ground turmeric
2 tablespoons fish sauce
¼ cup uncooked rice
3 tablespoons corn or peanut oil
2 tablespoons thin-sliced onion
1 garlic clove, sliced thin
½ inch of fresh ginger, sliced thin
1 stalk of lemongrass, cut into 3 pieces, pounded slightly to release
    aroma
5 cups water*

1. Rub the fish slices with turmeric and fish sauce.

2. Toast the rice in a dry skillet over low heat for 4 or 5 minutes, stirring frequently, until rice turns a light brown color. Do not burn.

3. Heat the oil in a pan and fry the onion over moderate heat until crisp and brown. Remove onion and set aside. Discard all but 1 tablespoon oil.

4. Fry the garlic and ginger in the same pan over moderate heat for 2 minutes. Add the lemongrass and fry for 1 minute more. Add the fish and its marinade and fry for 2 minutes. Add the rice and stir carefully for 2 minutes.

5. Add the water, bring to a boil, and cook over low heat for 20 minutes, or until the rice swells and becomes tender.

Serve warm. Sprinkle some of the crisp onion over each serving.

SERVES 4

NGA GAUNG CHIN YE

Fish Head Soup with Watercress

This soup is not attractive to look at but has an exceptionally appealing flavor. The heads of very large meaty fish are popular in Burma and extracting the small pockets of flesh is considered worth the effort.

Burmese use many kinds of aquatic plants not available to us. In this recipe they would use a variety of water spinach known as "rabbit greens" (*Ipomoea aquatica Forsk*), but watercress is an acceptable substitute.

> *1 fish head (about 1 pound tilefish, red snapper, or other meaty*
> *   fish), quartered*
> *2 tablespoons chopped onion*
> *1 garlic clove, chopped*
> *½ inch of fresh ginger, chopped*
> *½ teaspoon dried hot red chili flakes*
> *1 teaspoon paprika*
> *¼ teaspoon ground turmeric*
> *1 teaspoon shrimp paste*
> *2 teaspoons fish sauce*
> *1 teaspoon salt*
> *2 tablespoons corn or peanut oil*
> *4 cups water*
> *1 tablespoon tamarind paste, soaked in ¼ cup water, strained*
> *1 bunch of watercress, divided into sprigs*
> *¼ cup chopped fresh coriander*

1. Mix the fish head with the onion, garlic, ginger, chili flakes, paprika, turmeric, shrimp paste, fish sauce, salt, and oil. Lightly cook these in a pan over moderate heat for 10 minutes.

2. Add the water and tamarind liquid, bring to a boil, and cook in a covered pan over moderate heat for 20 minutes.

3. Add the watercress and coriander, cover the pan, and cook for 10 minutes more.

Serve hot with or without the pieces of fish head. Frequently served with plain white rice.

SERVES 4

GOBI TOAT HINCHO

Shrimp and Chinese Cabbage Soup

2 teaspoons corn or peanut oil
¼ cup thin-sliced onion
1 cup fresh shrimps, peeled, deveined, cut into ½-inch pieces
3 cups water
1 tablespoon fish sauce
¼ teaspoon salt
2 cups ¼-inch-wide slices of Chinese cabbage
2 scallions, sliced thin

1. Heat the oil in a pan and fry the onion over moderate heat for 1 minute. Add the shrimps and stir-fry for another minute. Add the water, fish sauce, and salt and bring to a boil. Cook for 2 minutes.

2. Add the cabbage and scallions and cook, covered, for 3 minutes more. Uncover and cook for 1 minute.

Serve hot.

SERVES 4

PAZUN HIN CHO

Clear Shrimp and Lime Soup

The subtle flavor of this soup results from both ingredients and method. The onion and ginger, cracked with the flat side of a cleaver, release their flavors into the broth along with the freshness of uncooked lime juice, chili, scallion, and coriander. The clear soup is ladled into individual bowls with a few shrimps, some coriander, and scallions. The Burmese have a saying: "When the shrimps curl up [in the soup] they are cooked."

4 cups water
12 jumbo shrimps, 1 pound, peeled and deveined
2 tablespoons fish sauce
2 tablespoons fresh lime juice
2 teaspoons soy sauce
1 small onion, quartered and cracked with a cleaver
1 slice of fresh ginger, cracked
2 tablespoons fresh semihot green chili, sliced
1 tablespoon sliced scallion
1 tablespoon coarse-chopped fresh coriander

1. Bring the water to a boil in a saucepan. Add the shrimps and fish sauce and simmer for 5 minutes.

2. In a soup tureen or serving bowl, put the lime juice, soy sauce, onion, ginger, chili, scallion, and coriander.

3. Pour the hot broth and shrimps over the ingredients in the bowl.

Serve immediately.

SERVES 4

MOHINGA

Classic Fish Soup with Garnishes

Mohinga is the national soup, served all over the country. This prep-aration is a classic, but there are variations depending on whether it is served near the sea where fish is cheap and plentiful or inland where it is not. Catfish is the most popular and traditional fish used.

In addition, simplified versions may be prepared by a drastic re-duction in the number of garnishes. In a small village compound, where I tasted the mohinga one morning, the only garnishes were one wide rice stick (noodle), halves of hard-cooked duck eggs, a few crispy onions, and hot chili flakes. It was still tasty but couldn't compare with the entire production using all the garnishes.

Although mohinga is sometimes served to large groups of people gathered for religious events, it is mainly a breakfast food. In the early morning hours, when the Burmese are going to work in the towns and cities, it is a common sight to see groups of people waiting to be served at corner restaurants. Large caldrons of mohinga are simmering and on a nearby table is the collection of garnishes. The diner may indicate whether hot chili is to be added as well as the ubiquitous fish sauce. Personal preference dictates the choice of flavoring.

SOUP CONCENTRATE

   4 pounds kingfish, catfish, cod, haddock, sea trout, or any meaty fish
   3 stalks of lemongrass, pounded to release aroma
   2 inches of fresh ginger, cracked with the side of a cleaver
   ½ teaspoon ground turmeric
   2 teaspoons shrimp paste
   3 tablespoons fish sauce
   7 whole dried long hot red chilies
   10 cups water

COMPLETE SOUP

   1 cup rice, toasted in a dry skillet until light brown, ground to a
       powder in a processor
   16 cups water
   3 tablespoons semolina (Cream of Wheat, soojee)
   ¼ cup roasted peanuts, ground to a powder in a processor
   ¼ cup corn or peanut oil

(continued on next page)

½ teaspoon ground turmeric
1 medium-size onion, sliced thin, ½ cup
2 garlic cloves, chopped fine
½ inch of fresh ginger, chopped fine
1 teaspoon paprika
1 teaspoon salt
3 tablespoons fish sauce
1 tablespoon sugar
1 can (1 pound) chick-peas, drained and processed to a paste with
    2 cups of the water
12 shallots, peeled

GARNISHES
1 pound white wheat spaghetti, Japanese-type, or No. 9
    supermarket spaghetti, cooked al dente according to package
    instructions
6 hard-cooked eggs, halved
1 recipe Split-Pea Fritters (Kalape Kyaw, see Index)
1 pound calabash, cut into 2-inch sticks and crisp-fried in Spicy
    Batter for Fried Vegetables (see Index)
1 fried fish cake, purchased in Asian grocery, or Basic Fish Cake
    (Nga Phe Kyaw, see Index)
½ cup Crispy Fried Onions (see Index)
3 scallions, sliced thin
¼ cup chopped fresh coriander
1 tablespoon dried hot red chili flakes, toasted lightly in a dry skillet
Lime slices
Fish sauce (optional)

1. Divide the whole fish into 2 pieces, cutting right through the bones. Put all the soup concentrate ingredients into a pan, bring to a boil, cover the pan, and cook over moderate heat for 30 minutes. Set aside and cool.

2. Carefully remove the fish from the broth and separate the meat from the bones. Discard the bones. Break the fish into small pieces. Strain and reserve the broth, discarding the lemongrass and other solids.

3. Mix the toasted rice powder with 2 cups of the water. Add the semolina and mix well. Add the peanut powder, mix, and let stand for 15 minutes.

4. Heat the oil in a pan large enough to contain the finished soup. Add the turmeric, onion, garlic, ginger, and paprika, and stir-fry over moderate heat for 2 minutes.

5. Add the boneless fish pieces and stir-fry for 5 minutes. Add the salt, fish sauce, and sugar. Stir well.

6. Add the chick-pea paste, the rice/semolina paste, and the reserved broth from the soup concentrate. Add the balance of the water (12 cups). Add the shallots last. Bring the soup to a boil and simmer over *low* heat for 1 hour. Stir frequently.

7. When ready to serve, put about ½ cup of the spaghetti in each soup bowl. On top of that, place ½ hard-cooked egg, 1 tablespoon split pea fritter, broken up, 3 calabash stick halves, 1 slice of fish cake, 1 teaspoon each of crispy onion, scallion, and coriander, ¼ teaspoon hot chili flakes, or to taste. Pour 1 cup hot fish soup over all and add lime juice to taste, and fish sauce if desired.

SERVES 10 TO 12

Note: In Burma, the banana stem, known as *ngapyaw* or "banana intestine," is an important ingredient in the *mohinga*. The round stem is cut into ⅛-inch-thick slices and added to the soup. It has the texture of crispy celery and does not dissolve during long simmering. We have substituted shallots.

PYI-BYI NGA CHIN HIN

Lemon-Flavored Vegetable Soup with Squid

This excellent soup has an abundance of textures and flavors and is easy to assemble. It tastes as good the second day after being simply rewarmed. Be sure not to overcook or the squid will become rubbery.

½ pound squid, dressed and cut into 1-inch pieces
4 cups boiling water
1 teaspoon salt
2 cups ¼-inch-wide slices of Chinese cabbage
1 cup 2-inch pieces of green snap beans
½ cup chopped fresh or canned tomatoes
1 teaspoon paprika
2 teaspoons soy sauce
1 teaspoon fish sauce
1 scallion, sliced into ½-inch pieces
2 tablespoons chopped fresh coriander
3 inches semihot chili, halved lengthwise
1 tablespoon lemon or lime juice

1. Cook the squid in the water and salt for 2 minutes. Remove squid with a slotted spoon and set aside.

2. Add the cabbage, snap beans, tomatoes, paprika, soy sauce, and fish sauce to the squid broth and cook in a covered pan over moderate heat for 5 minutes.

3. Return squid to the broth and cook for 2 minutes. Add the scallion, coriander, chili, and lemon juice. Stir for a moment.

Serve hot.

SERVES 4

BEEF AND LAMB

Beef, buffalo, and mutton or lamb cannot be considered important and popular meats in Burma, principally due to their price and availability. Price is high and availability low, in part because of religious convictions. The Buddhists abhor killing any animal, and the bigger the animal the more serious is the sin. They must look to Muslim butchers for this task. The Chinese butchers slaughter pigs and ducks especially, but other poultry as well.

In spite of this, the beef recipes they have concocted cannot be faulted for their pungent seasonings and imaginative combinations. Most of them are of Indo-Burmese origin, usually in the form of curries—another manifestation of the influence of India and China on the Burmese cuisine.

Some of the mountain people, especially the Burmese of Indian origin, eat lamb and mutton, but they are few in proportion and the recipes limited in number.

AMETHA PUDEENA

Beef and Mint

This beef dish can have as much chili sting as you wish by adjusting the amount used. The word *pudeena* is actually Indian, but is used in Burma to denote mint.

1 pound beef chuck, cut into ½-inch cubes
1 cup water
¼ teaspoon salt
¼ teaspoon ground turmeric
2 teaspoons corn or peanut oil
1 garlic clove, chopped
¼ teaspoon ground cuminseed
½ cup sliced onion
½ cup quartered tomatoes, fresh or canned
2 teaspoons soy sauce
3 or 4 fresh hot green chilies (to taste), sliced
1 cup loosely packed fresh mint leaves

1. Cook the beef in the water with salt and turmeric over moderately low heat for about 1 hour, or until the beef is tender and almost all the liquid has evaporated. Set aside.

2. In a wok or skillet, heat the oil and stir-fry the garlic over moderate heat for 1 minute. Add the cuminseed, onion, and tomatoes, and stir-fry for 3 minutes.

3. Add the tender beef, the soy sauce, chilies, and mint, and stir-fry for 3 minutes.

Serve warm with other dishes.

SERVES 4 TO 6

Variation: Boneless lamb cubes may be used as a substitute for beef. In fact, lamb and mint are an extremely compatible combination.

JU-BU AMETHA KYAW
Beef and Indian Leek Stir-Fry

2 teaspoons corn or peanut oil
⅛ teaspoon ground turmeric
1 tablespoon onion slices
½ teaspoon sugar
6 ounces sirloin or flank steak, sliced julienne
2 cups Indian leeks, green part with seed pods only, cut into 2-inch
    pieces
2 teaspoons soy sauce
½ teaspoon salt
½ cup sweet red pepper, sliced julienne

1. Heat the oil in a wok or skillet. Add the turmeric, onion, and sugar, and stir-fry over moderate heat until the onion is light brown, about 3 minutes.

2. Add the beef and stir-fry for 2 minutes; add the leeks and stir-fry for 2 minutes. Add the soy sauce, salt, and red pepper, and stir-fry for 2 minutes more, to blend the flavorings.

Serve warm with other dishes.

SERVES 4

Variation: It may not always be possible to find the crunchy Indian leeks complete with their pods. As a substitute, the Chinese long bean, cut into 1-inch pieces, may be used since it has similar texture. Or garlic chives with the bud attached may be substituted. They are usually available in Chinatowns.

ON NO AMETHA HNAT

Beef "Slow-Cook" in Coconut Milk

3 fresh coconuts
3 teaspoons salt
2 medium-size onions, sliced, 1 cup
2 garlic cloves, sliced
½ inch of fresh ginger, sliced
2 teaspoons paprika
2 tablespoons corn or peanut oil
2 pounds beef chuck, cut into 2-inch pieces

1. Prepare homemade Coconut Milk (see Index) with 3 coconuts, 1 teaspoon of the salt, and 7 cups hot water. Make 2 cups coconut milk as the first pressing and 5 cups coconut milk in the second pressing, both with hot water.

2. Crush together in a processor the onions, garlic, ginger, and paprika to make a smooth paste. Mix this spice mixture with remaining 2 teaspoons salt, the oil, and the beef cubes. Marinate for 30 minutes.

3. Put the beef and spice mixture in a pan and over moderate heat brown the beef. After about 15 minutes of frying and stirring, add the 5 cups coconut milk from the second pressing. Bring to a boil and cook, covered, for about 1 hour. The liquid will have almost evaporated.

4. Add the 2 cups coconut milk from the first pressing. Cook for 20 to 25 minutes more, to tenderize the beef completely. The sauce will become thick, rich, and slightly oily from the coconut milk.

Serve warm with rice or bread, salads, and chutneys.

SERVES 6

Variation: Boneless cubes of lamb may be used instead of the beef. A Burmese friend has told me that it is even tastier than beef.

AMETHA PYOAT KYAW

Boiled Fried Beef

This crisp beef is first boiled in water, then fried in oil, all in the same pan. This is a method often used in Burma. The beef can then be refrigerated for 1 week and the seasoned oil used for other purposes.

*2 pounds boneless beef chuck, cut into pieces 2 inches long and ¼
    inch thick*
1 teaspoon salt
1 tablespoon soy sauce
⅛ teaspoon ground turmeric
1 cup water
1 cup corn or peanut oil

1. Mix everything together. Bring to a boil over moderate heat. Cook in a half-covered pan until the water evaporates, about 1 hour.

2. Continue to brown the beef in the oil that remains for 10 minutes more. Remove the beef with a slotted spoon.

Serve warm, at room temperature, or cold as a snack with drinks.

SERVES 6

AMETHA HIN

Beef in Tamarind Sauce

The literal translation of this standard beef dish is "Beef Curry in a Tamarind Sauce." Curry is a convenient catchall word much used in Burma and does not necessarily refer to an Indian curry. It is really a holdover from British Colonial times.

1 medium-size onion, sliced, ½ cup
2 garlic cloves, sliced
1 inch of fresh ginger, sliced
1½ cups water
1 pound boneless beef chuck, cut into 2-inch pieces
1 teaspoon salt
2 tablespoons corn or peanut oil
2 teaspoons fish sauce
¼ teaspoon ground turmeric
1 teaspoon paprika
1 heaping teaspoon tamarind paste, dissolved in ½ cup water and
*   strained through a metal sieve*

1. Process the onion, garlic, ginger, and ¼ cup of the water to a coarse paste. Put the paste, beef, salt, oil, fish sauce, turmeric, and paprika in a pan and mix well. Let this stand for 15 minutes.

2. Cook the beef, covered, over moderate heat for 15 minutes. Stir well and add the balance of the water, 1¼ cups. Bring to a boil and cook the beef until tender, about 1 hour.

3. Add the tamarind liquid and cook for 10 minutes more.

Serve warm with rice.

SERVES 4

AMEHNAT

Country-Style Beef

This dish is known as a "slow cook" and is prepared over wood fires in the villages. Keeping the pan covered and simmering slowly ensures that the flavors are sealed in. It is a typical method of village cooking.

MARINADE

1 medium-size onion, chopped fine, ½ cup
1 large garlic clove, chopped fine
½ inch of fresh ginger, chopped fine
1 teaspoon dried hot red chili flakes
½ teaspoon salt
2 teaspoons fish sauce
¼ teaspoon ground turmeric
1 tablespoon corn or peanut oil

1 pound boneless beef chuck, cut into 2-inch cubes
1 cup water
1 stalk of lemongrass, cut into 4 pieces, lightly pounded
1 teaspoon tamarind paste, dissolved in 2 tablespoons water,
   strained through a metal sieve

1. Mix marinade ingredients together; pour over beef, and marinate for 15 minutes.

2. Put the beef and marinade in a pan, add the water and lemongrass, and stir to mix. Bring to a boil, cover, and simmer over low heat for about 1½ hours. Do not uncover the pan until beef is almost tender. Shake the pan once or twice during this time.

3. When the beef is tender, add the tamarind liquid; adjust the salt if necessary. Cook the beef for 5 minutes more.

Serve warm with rice and other dishes.

SERVES 4 TO 6

AME-HNAT

Beef "Slow-Cook"

½ cup corn or peanut oil
⅛ teaspoon ground turmeric
1 cup thin-sliced onions
2 pounds round steak or boneless chuck, cut into 2-inch cubes
2 tablespoons sour cream
2 teaspoons fish sauce
1 teaspoon salt
1 teaspoon ground cuminseed
2 teaspoons paprika
1 teaspoon fine-chopped fresh ginger
2 garlic cloves, chopped fine
1 cup water

1. Heat the oil in a pan and add the turmeric. Add the onions and fry them crisp over moderate heat; do not burn. Remove onions and set aside. Remove all the oil except 2 tablespoons.

2. Marinate the beef for 1 to 2 hours in the sour cream, fish sauce, salt, cuminseed, paprika, and the reserved fried onions, all mixed well together.

3. Heat the reserved 2 tablespoons oil in the same pan and brown the ginger and garlic over moderate heat for 2 minutes. Add the marinated beef mixture and brown well for 15 to 20 minutes. Stir frequently.

4. Add the water, cover the pan, and cook over low heat for about 1½ hours, until beef is tender. The sauce will have reduced to a thick consistency.

Serve warm with rice, Indian breads, and especially with the 100-Layer Pancakes (Htad-Taya, see Index).

SERVES 6

AMETHA KABAB
Beef, Mint, and Cumin Stir-Fry

The culinary influence of Burma's neighbors is apparent in a recipe now and then, but often these imports become Burmanized to such an extent that they end up being more Burmese than foreign. In this title, "kabab" for instance reveals an Indian origin, but the preparation is definitely Burmese.

1 tablespoon corn or peanut oil
1 medium-size onion, sliced, ½ cup
¼ teaspoon ground turmeric
1 medium-size green pepper, cut into ½-inch cubes, about 1 cup
1 medium-size ripe tomato, cut into ½-inch cubes, ½ cup
½ teaspoon salt
1 tablespoon soy sauce
2 cups ½-inch cubes cooked roast or boiled beef
1 teaspoon ground cuminseed
2 scallions, sliced
½ cup loosely packed fresh mint leaves

1. Heat the oil in a wok or large skillet and stir-fry the onion and turmeric over moderate heat for 1 minute. Add the green pepper and stir-fry for 1 minute. Add the tomato, salt, soy sauce, and beef and stir-fry for 3 minutes.

2. Add the cuminseed and scallions, continuing to stir-fry. Lastly, add the mint and cover the wok for 2 minutes. Uncover, and stir-fry for 1 minute more.

Serve warm with coconut rice or varieties of white bread.

SERVES 4

ATHALON HIN

Meatball Curry

This is a fine preparation that can be made in any quantity for a group of any size. It may be made the day before using, which will only enhance the flavor.

1 pound ground beef
2 teaspoons rice flour
⅛ teaspoon ground turmeric
½ teaspoon salt
½ teaspoon paprika
1 teaspoon fish sauce
1 tablespoon sliced semihot green chili
1 teaspoon fresh ginger, crushed
1 large garlic clove, crushed
1 medium-size onion, crushed, about ½ cup
2 tablespoons corn or peanut oil
½ stalk of lemongrass, slightly pounded
½ teaspoon dried hot red chili flakes
½ cup chopped ripe tomatoes, fresh or canned
2 teaspoons tamarind paste, dissolved in ¼ cup water, strained
1 cup water

1. Mix together the beef, rice flour, turmeric, salt, paprika, fish sauce, and green chili. Scoop up the ginger, garlic, and onion, which have been chopped very fine together in a processor, and squeeze the liquid over the beef. Mix well and reserve the ginger/garlic/onion pulp.

2. Prepare meatballs 1 inch in diameter and slightly flattened on both ends. Makes about 20.

3. Heat the oil in a pan and lightly brown the meatballs on both sides over moderate heat for 2 minutes. Remove and set aside.

4. In the same oil, fry the ginger/garlic/onion pulp, the lemongrass, and chili flakes over moderate heat for 2 minutes. Add the tomatoes and stir-fry for 2 minutes more.

5. Add the meatballs, tamarind liquid, and water, and cook the curry over moderately low heat for 15 minutes, or a bit more to thicken the sauce.

Serve warm with rice, salad, and other Burmese dishes.

SERVES 4 TO 6

ATHA-LON KIN

Ground Beef Barbecue

This Indo-Burmese recipe lends itself especially to summer outdoor barbecues, but it should also be considered for a fat-free, well-seasoned grill in a gas or electric broiler.

1 pound ground beef
½ cup loosely packed chopped fresh mint leaves
1 teaspoon crushed fresh ginger
2 garlic cloves, crushed
½ teaspoon salt
2 teaspoons soy sauce
7 bamboo skewers, soaked in water for 1 hour

1. Mix everything together except the skewers.

2. Shape meatballs 1 inch in diameter. Slip five of them onto each skewer, ½ inch apart. Broil over charcoal or in an oven broiler for about 5 minutes.

Serve warm.

SERVES 4

Variation: Ground pork or lamb may be used instead of beef, but when pork is used it should be cooked longer, about 8 to 10 minutes, to ensure that it is cooked all the way through. The other ingredients are the same.

AMETHE LON ALOO

Meatballs and Potatoes

This is straightforward home cooking of the most appetizing kind. It glorifies traditional European ingredients—meat and potatoes—with the flavorings of Burma.

> 1 pound ground beef
> ¼ teaspoon salt
> 1 tablespoon soy sauce
> 1 teaspoon rice flour
> Oil for deep-frying
> ½ pound potatoes (2 medium-size), peeled, cut into ½-inch cubes
> 1 small onion, chopped, ¼ cup
> 1 garlic clove, chopped
> ½ inch of fresh ginger, chopped
> ¼ teaspoon ground turmeric
> 1 teaspoon ground cuminseed
> 1 teaspoon paprika
> 1 small ripe tomato, cut into ½-inch cubes
> 1 scallion, sliced thin
> 1 teaspoon chopped fresh hot green chili
> 2 tablespoons water

1. Mix the beef with the salt, 1 teaspoon of the soy sauce, and rice flour. Prepare meatballs ¾ inch in diameter. Set aside.

2. Heat the oil in a skillet and fry the potato cubes over moderate heat until brown, about 6 minutes. Remove them and set aside. Remove all but 2 tablespoons oil.

3. In the same skillet brown the meatballs for 2 minutes. Remove them and set aside.

4. Fry the onion, garlic, ginger, and turmeric over moderate heat for 2 minutes. Add the cuminseed, paprika, and the remaining 2 teaspoons soy sauce, and stir-fry for 1 minute.

5. Add the tomato, then the meatballs, and mix. Add the browned potato cubes, the scallion and chili and mix well. Add the water and cook for 2 minutes more.

Serve warm with bread or rice.

SERVES 4

KYET-HIN-KHA ASA THUT

Beef-Stuffed Bitter Melon

4 ounces ground beef
¼ cup chopped onion
1 garlic clove, chopped
1 teaspoon chopped fresh ginger
1 teaspoon chopped fresh hot green chili
4 teaspoons fish sauce
2 bitter melons, about 1 pound
2 teaspoons corn or peanut oil
¼ cup water

1. Mix the beef, onion, garlic, ginger, chili, and 2 teaspoons fish sauce together. Let stand for 15 minutes.

2. Cut the melons lengthwise into halves and trim off ¼ inch from each end. Scoop out and discard the seeds and pulp.

3. Stuff half of each melon with beef mixture, top with the other half, and tie together with string.

4. Put the melons into a pan. Add the oil, remaining 2 teaspoons fish sauce, and the water. Cover the pan and cook over moderate heat for 10 minutes. Turn the melons over and cook for 10 minutes more. Should the pan dry out too quickly, add 1 or 2 tablespoons water.

Remove the strings and cut each melon into 4 pieces.
Serve warm with other dishes.

SERVES 4

Variations: Fresh shrimps, peeled, deveined, and coarsely chopped, are a good substitute for beef. Ground pork may also be used instead of beef. The same amounts and flavoring will be agreeable should you prefer to substitute.

AMETHE SOAT NAN NAN PIN

Beef Pattie with Coriander

PATTIE
> 1 pound ground beef
> ¼ teaspoon ground turmeric
> ¼ teaspoon paprika
> ½ teaspoon salt
> 1 tablespoon rice flour
> 1 teaspoon fish sauce
> 2 tablespoons corn or peanut oil

GRAVY
> ½ cup thin-sliced onion
> 1 garlic clove, chopped
> ¼ teaspoon ground turmeric
> ¼ teaspoon paprika
> ½ teaspoon salt
> 1 teaspoon ground cuminseed
> ½ cup ½-inch cubes of sweet red pepper
> ¼ cup chopped tomato, fresh or canned
> 2 teaspoons soy sauce
> ½ cup water
> 2 scallions, sliced thin
> 6 stalks of fresh coriander, cut into 1-inch pieces, about ½ cup

1. Mix together the beef, turmeric, paprika, salt, rice flour, and fish sauce. Prepare patties 2½ inches in diameter and about ¼ inch thick, or a bit more.

2. Heat the oil in a skillet and brown the patties over moderate heat for 2 minutes on each side. Remove and set aside.

3. In the same skillet brown the onion and garlic over moderate heat for 3 minutes. Add the turmeric, paprika, salt, and cuminseed, and stir-fry for 1 minute. Add the red pepper, tomato, and soy sauce, and stir-fry for 2 minutes.

4. Add the water and the browned patties, cover the skillet, and cook over moderately low heat for 5 minutes. Uncover the skillet and sprinkle with scallion slices and coriander pieces.

Serve warm with other dishes.

SERVES 4

OO-HNAUK HIN

Spiced Brain

This Indo-Burmese recipe shows the influence of India from the spices and yogurt used. It is not a real curry but a dish using flavorings preferred by the Burmese.

> 1 beef brain, about 1 pound
> 1 teaspoon salt
> 2 teaspoons soy sauce
> 2 rounded tablespoons plain yogurt
> 2 tablespoons corn or peanut oil
> 2 garlic cloves, chopped fine
> ½ inch of fresh ginger, chopped fine
> 1 medium-size onion, chopped fine, ½ cup
> ⅛ teaspoon ground turmeric
> ½ teaspoon paprika
> 1 teaspoon ground cuminseed
> 1 tablespoon poppy seeds, crushed in a mortar
> 1 medium-size tomato, quartered

1. Soak the brain in cold water and carefully remove the outer membrane. Cut the brain into 1-inch cubes.

2. Sprinkle the salt, soy sauce, and yogurt over the brain and mix everything together.

3. Heat the oil in a skillet and add the garlic, ginger, and onion. Stir-fry over moderate heat for 2 minutes. Add the turmeric, paprika, cuminseed, and poppy seeds, and stir-fry for 1 minute. Add the tomato and stir-fry for 2 minutes longer.

4. Add the brain, mix well, and fry for 5 minutes, turning the mixture now and then.

Serve warm with rice or bread.

SERVES 4

AME-KALEZA

Beef Innards in Lemongrass Sauce

This is a village style of preparation where the whole animal (whether it is beef, pork, lamb, or goat) is utilized in a tasty and traditional way.

1 stalk of lemongrass, cut into halves and cracked with flat of blade
1 medium-size onion, chopped, ½ cup
2 garlic cloves, chopped fine
1 inch of fresh ginger, chopped fine
2 tablespoons fish sauce
⅛ teaspoon ground tumeric
1 teaspoon salt
2 teaspoons paprika
1 fresh semihot green chili, sliced thin
2 tablespoons oil

BEEF

½ pound cleaned cooked tripe, cut into 1½-inch pieces
½ pound heart, cut into 1-inch cubes
½ pound liver, cut into 1-inch cubes
½ pound boneless chuck, cut into 1-inch cubes

2½ cups water

1. Mix all the flavorings and oil together and marinate the meats in the mixture for 30 minutes.

2. Fry the mixture in a pan over moderate heat for 20 minutes, stirring frequently.

3. Add the water, cover, and cook over moderately low heat for about 1 hour. The liquid will have been reduced to a thick gravy and the meats should be tender.

Serve warm with rice or bread and with other dishes.

SERVES 6

SEIK THA KIN

Barbecued Lamb Chops

1 pound shoulder lamb chops
¼ teaspoon ground turmeric
¼ teaspoon salt
¼ teaspoon ground pepper

MARINADE

1 teaspoon ground cuminseed
1 teaspoon paprika
1 teaspoon honey
1 teaspoon lemon juice
2 teaspoons soy sauce

1. Cut each chop into halves and rub the lamb pieces with the turmeric, salt, and pepper. Let stand for 15 minutes.

2. Mix marinade ingredients together. Set aside.

3. Broil the lamb in an oven broiler for 2 minutes or, better still, grill over charcoal. Paint the broiled side with half of the marinade. Turn the lamb over and paint the other side. Complete the broiling for 3 to 5 minutes more.

Serve warm with lemon slices and trimmed scallions.

SERVES 4

SEIK-THA GHOP

Twice-Cooked Lamb Chop

This is an Anglo-Burmese dish, with Burmese spices mild enough to suit the English palate. Very tasty indeed, and easy to prepare. Large shoulder chops may be divided.

1½ pounds rib or shoulder chops, divided into 6 or 7 pieces
2 inches of fresh ginger, chopped
⅛ teaspoon ground turmeric
1 teaspoon salt
1 teaspoon soy sauce
1 cup water
¼ cup corn or peanut oil
2 eggs, beaten

1. In a covered pan, cook the chops, ginger, turmeric, salt, and soy sauce in the water over moderate heat for about 15 minutes, until the water evaporates. Remove the chops; cool.

2. Heat the oil in a skillet. Dip each chop into the beaten egg and brown it over moderate heat for about 5 minutes. Drain on paper towels.

Serve warm with a dip.

SERVES 4

PORK

It is surprising that in a hot, tropical country like Burma, the most popular meat is pork. But there are several good reasons for this.

First, in the Shan State in Upper Burma, there is a large Chinese population, and they are traditionally great pork eaters. Then, another surprise, although the Lord Buddha died of eating tainted pork some 2,500 years ago, his followers have not been discouraged by this and so the Buddhists are also fond of pork. It is only the Muslims who abstain.

Pork is much cheaper than beef or lamb and, finally, it has such versatility in combining with a wide variety of other foods and seasonings that it is a challenge to Burmese ingenuity. Each recipe in our collection is unusual and flavorful, whether it is an appetizer or an important festival dish. So, for those aficionados of pork, a real treat is in store.

WETTHA APO-DTHATSA

Diet Pork

Pork prepared in this manner is recommended by Buddhist healers for persons who are watching their diet (*tha-moat-htan*). And for all of us this simple dish has appeal because, although flavorful, it is prepared without fat and is not overly spicy. It makes a tasty appetizer served with a dip, or it may be served as a side dish.

1 pound boneless lean pork, cut into 1-inch cubes
1½ cups water
2 teaspoons palm sugar, Indian jaggery, or commercial brown sugar
1 teaspoon tamarind paste, dissolved in 2 tablespoons water,
    strained
½ teaspoon salt
1 teaspoon fish sauce

1. Cook the pork in the water in a covered pan over moderate heat for about 45 minutes, until the liquid has nearly evaporated.

2. Add the sugar, tamarind liquid, salt, and fish sauce. Cook over low heat until almost all the liquid has evaporated and just enough sauce remains so that the pork is moist.

Serve warm with rice with other dishes.

SERVES 4

WETTHANI HIN

Red Pork Pot Roast

This is not a special kind of pork but only called "red" because the caramelized sugar turns the pork a reddish brown. In Rangoon the cooks are apt to use a 12-ounce bottle of beer in place of the water to add extra flavor. Out in the country, where life is simpler, some cooks prefer to use liquor (firewater), which also effectively improves the flavor.

2 pounds boneless pork, cut into 2-inch pieces
2 tablespoons soy sauce
½ teaspoon salt
2 tablespoons corn or peanut oil
1 tablespoon white or brown sugar
2 garlic cloves, sliced
1 inch of fresh ginger, chopped
2 cups water

1. Marinate the pork in the soy sauce and salt for 1 hour.

2. Heat the oil in a pan, add the sugar, and stir over heat for a moment to caramelize the sugar. Add the garlic and ginger and stir-fry over moderate heat until brown, about 2 minutes.

3. Add the pork and mix well. Cover the pan and cook for 15 minutes, stirring every now and then.

4. Add the water, cover, and continue to cook for 45 minutes, or until the pork is tender and the liquid has almost evaporated.

Serve warm or at room temperature.

SERVES 6

SI CHET KYAUK SWE

Roast Pork and Garlic Noodles

This noodle style is a specialty of the big towns, such as Rangoon and Mandalay. It is food sold by hawkers or prepared in restaurants. It is seldom cooked at home. In New York, I buy the special roast pork in Chinatown.

> *1 pound fresh egg noodles*
> *3 tablespoons Garlic Oil (see Index)*
> *2 tablespoons soy sauce*
> *½ teaspoon salt*
> *¼ teaspoon pepper*
> *½ pound Chinese roast pork, cut into slices 1 inch long and ¼ inch thick*
> *Tabasco or other bottled hot sauce*

1. Drop the egg noodles into boiling water and cook over moderate heat for 3 minutes. Drain the noodles and rinse under cold water.

2. Mix the noodles with the oil, soy sauce, salt, and pepper, and toss well. Garnish with the roast pork and splash on your favorite hot sauce to taste.

Serve at room temperature.

SERVES 4 TO 6

MONHNYIN WETTHA KYAW

Pork and Swiss Chard Stir-Fry

> *¼ pound boneless pork, cut into ¼-inch-thick julienne pieces*
> *3 teaspoons soy sauce*
> *¼ teaspoon salt*
> *1 tablespoon corn or peanut oil*
> *1 garlic clove, chopped fine*
> *1 cup 2-inch-long Swiss chard stems*
> *4 cups 2-inch-wide Swiss chard leaf slices*

1. Marinate pork in 1 teaspoon soy sauce and the salt for about 1 hour.

2. Heat the oil in a wok or skillet and stir-fry the garlic over moderate heat for 1 minute. Add the pork and stir-fry for 3 minutes or a bit more to cook thoroughly.

3. Add the chard stems and fry for 1 minute. Add the rest of the soy sauce and stir-fry for another 2 minutes. Add the chard leaves and fry for 2 to 3 minutes more, just to combine the flavors and wilt the leaves; do not overcook.

Serve warm with rice with other dishes.

SERVES 4

WETTHA NANATHI HIN

Pork and Pineapple

2 pounds boneless pork, cut into 2-inch cubes
3 tablespoons chopped onion
1 tablespoon chopped garlic
2 teaspoons chopped fresh ginger
1 tablespoon paprika, or 2 teaspoons dried hot red chili flakes
½ teaspoon salt
2 tablespoons fish sauce
1 cup pineapple cubes, fresh ripe or canned
2 tablespoons corn or peanut oil
2 cups water

1. Mix all ingredients except the water together in a pan and marinate for 15 minutes.

2. Cook the mixture in a covered pan over moderate heat for 20 minutes.

3. Add the water, bring to a boil, and cook for 45 minutes, or until the pork is firm but tender and the sauce has reduced to about ½ cup.

Serve warm with rice and salad.

SERVES 6

WETTHA O-GYI CHET

Big Caldron Pork

This is a popular curry served in country villages whenever there is a ceremony to which all the inhabitants are invited. It is especially popular when young novices are to be inducted into the Buddhist fraternity and don the yellow robes of a monk. During the period of this initiation of the novitiates (*shin-byu*), the entire village cooperates to prepare and serve the pork in whatever large quantities are needed. It is because of the large quantities made that it is given the name of "big caldron" cooking.

3 pounds boneless pork, fresh shoulder or ham with skin, fat, and
*   meat, cut into 3-inch pieces*
1 medium-size onion, chopped, ½ cup
1 garlic clove, chopped
½ inch of fresh ginger, chopped
1 tablespoon dried hot red chili flakes
1 teaspoon salt
1 tablespoon fish sauce
1 tablespoon corn or peanut oil
4 cups water

1. Put everything except the water into a pan and cook over moderate heat for 15 minutes to brown the pork.

2. Add the water, bring to a boil, cover, and simmer over low heat for 2½ hours. Nearly all the liquid will evaporate and the pork will become quite tender.

Serve warm with rice.

SERVES 6

WETTHA THAYET THI CHET

Pork with Green Mango

Green mango is a meat tenderizer as well as a flavoring. For best results, the mango should be still sour, not ripe. Since the skin is tender, it may be grated with the pulp. The number of ingredients used here is small and so the success of the preparation depends on thoroughly browning the flavorings and pork.

1 medium-size onion, cut into ½-inch slices
1 inch of fresh ginger, sliced
3 garlic cloves, sliced
¼ cup corn or peanut oil
2 teaspoons dried hot red chili flakes
¼ teaspoon ground turmeric
1 teaspoon shrimp paste
2 teaspoons shrimp sauce
2 pounds boneless pork, cut into 2-inch pieces
½ cup grated green unripened mango (grated with skin)
1 teaspoon salt
2 cups water

1. Crush the onion, ginger, and garlic into a paste in a mortar.

2. Heat the oil in a pan and stir-fry the paste, the chili flakes, and turmeric over moderate heat for 5 minutes or more, to develop a reddish-brown color. Add the shrimp paste and shrimp sauce and continue to stir-fry for 2 minutes more.

3. Add the pork, green mango, and salt and continue to fry the mixture for about 10 minutes, until the pork is thoroughly brown.

4. Add the water, cover the pan, and cook over moderately low heat for 45 minutes. The oil will rise to indicate the pork is cooked, and the sauce will be reduced to a thick, rich brown paste.

Serve warm with other dishes and white rice.

SERVES 6

WETHA ATONE PAUNG

Well-Browned Steamed Pork

This dish is a Sino-Shan recipe from the Shan State in eastern Burma near the border of China. It is prepared by the Chinese people of that region and is sometimes known as "Wet Stew."

5 pounds fresh ham, with bone
4 tablespoons soy sauce
2 tablespoons salt
2 tablespoons brown sugar
2 tablespoons pale dry sherry or rice wine
½ inch of fresh ginger, sliced
2 garlic cloves, sliced

1. Rinse the ham with cold water and dry it. Rub it with 2 tablespoons soy sauce and 1 tablespoon salt and let it stand for a minimum of 2 hours. Overnight is better.

2. Mix remaining soy sauce and salt with the sugar, sherry, ginger, and garlic, and set aside.

3. In an oven broiler, or over charcoal in a barbecue, broil the ham on all sides for about 15 minutes to brown the skin.

4. Put the ham in a heatproof glass dish or bowl with the sugar/wine mixture. Steam over hot water in a Chinese-style steamer for 2½ to 3 hours. The meat will pull away easily from the bone when ready. On the other hand, a pressure cooker works very well; if you use it, the time for cooking is reduced to 1 hour.

Serve warm with white rice and a medley of other Burmese dishes.

SERVES 8

Note: You may wish to try this interesting fat-free preparation using a smaller piece of meat. For a fresh ham half the size of the one called for in this recipe, just reduce all the other ingredients by half. Cooking time will be the same.

PONYE GYI WETTHA HIN

Pork Stew in Black Bean Sauce

This is an extraordinary pork concoction, certainly one of my favorites. The pungent black-bean sauce together with the marinated pork make a very happy combination.

2 pounds boneless pork with some rind, cut into 2-inch cubes
1 medium-size onion, chopped, ½ cup
5 garlic cloves, chopped
1 inch of fresh ginger, chopped
1 tablespoon paprika, or 2 teaspoons dried hot red chili flakes
1 teaspoon shrimp paste
3 tablespoons fish sauce
1 cup Fermented Black Bean Paste (Pagan Ponyee Gyi, see Index)
2 tablespoons corn or peanut oil
2½ cups water

1. Mix everything together with ½ cup of the water and marinate for 15 minutes.

2. Bring the mixture to a boil and cook in a covered pan over moderate heat for 20 minutes.

3. Add remaining 2 cups water, bring again to a boil, and cook, covered, over moderate heat for 45 minutes, or until the pork is tender. The sauce will reduce to about 1 cup—rich, thick, and black.

Serve warm.

SERVES 6

SHWE PAYON THI WETTHA

Pork and Pumpkin Stew

   2 pounds boneless pork, cut into 2-inch cubes
   1 tablespoon soy sauce
   1 teaspoon salt
   1 tablespoon minced ginger
   1 tablespoon minced garlic
   ½ cup chopped onion
   ½ teaspoon ground turmeric
   2 tablespoons corn or peanut oil
   1 teaspoon shrimp paste
   2 teaspoons dried hot red chili flakes
   2 cups water
   1 pound pumpkin or butternut squash, cut into 2-inch cubes

1. Marinate the pork with soy sauce and salt for 1 hour.

2. In a large saucepan, place the pork and marinade, the ginger, garlic, onion, turmeric, oil, shrimp paste, hot chili flakes, and 1 cup water. Mix well and bring to a boil over moderate heat. Cover the pan and cook for 40 minutes.

3. Add the balance of water and the pumpkin. Cook for 15 minutes or more, until the pork is tender and the liquid has nearly evaporated. The pumpkin should be soft but not disintegrating.

Serve warm with white rice.

SERVES 6

WETTHA LEIK

Pork Roll

An appetizer with character, the whole pork roll can be prepared early in the day and briefly reheated in a 350°F. oven. It is then sliced with scissors and served. Traditionally, the pork strips are wrapped with the net of caul fat from pork. However, in the interests of health, I have substituted spring-roll wrappers to hold the meat strips together.

BATTER

> ½ cup Toasted Chick-Pea Flour (Besan, see Index)
> ½ cup glutinous rice flour
> ¾ cup cold water

PORK

> 1 pound boneless pork shoulder
> 1 inch of fresh ginger, cracked
> 1 teaspoon salt
> 1 cup water

> 1 package Chinese spring-roll wrappers
> Oil for deep-frying

1. Mix batter ingredients together until smooth.

2. Put pork with ginger, salt, and water into a pan, cover, and cook over moderately low heat until the water evaporates, about 30 minutes. Cool the pork and cut into 8 strips 4 inches long and ½ inch wide.

3. Place 2 pork strips alongside each other on a roll wrapper. Fold the wrapper in half and fold over the sides to make a roll 5 inches long and 2 inches wide.

4. Dip the roll into the batter.

5. Heat the oil in a skillet and brown the roll on all sides over moderate heat for 4 minutes. Drain on paper towel briefly. Cut the roll with scissors into 1-inch-wide slices.

Serve warm or at room temperature with Red Chili Dip (Nga Yok Chin, see Index).

MAKES 4 PORK ROLLS

Note: Roll extra wrappers in plastic food wrap and store in a damp cloth. Otherwise they will dry out very quickly.

HIN-DOK

Curry Packet

In Burma, this pork is wrapped in banana leaves and fastened with a wooden skewer. Although the foil is adequate for cooking purposes, the banana leaf does impart a pleasant aroma to the mixture. Since it is now possible to purchase, in New York's Chinatown, packages of frozen banana leaves imported from Thailand, you may like to use them. Place a strip of leaf 4 inches wide and about 10 inches long in the middle of the foil square. Put the pork mixture in the center of this and fold over. This will give the food a more traditional flavor.

2 pounds boneless pork, including some pork skin
1 cup rice flour
4 scallions, cut into ½-inch-wide pieces
1 medium-size onion, chopped fine, ½ cup
2 garlic cloves, chopped fine
1 inch of fresh ginger, chopped fine
2 tablespoons soy sauce
1 teaspoon salt
1 semihot green chili, sliced thin
1 teaspoon corn or peanut oil
⅛ teaspoon ground turmeric
½ teaspoon paprika
½ cup water

Aluminum foil, cut into 12-inch squares

1. Cut the pork into pieces about ¼ inch thick and 1 inch square.

2. Mix the pork with all the other ingredients (the mixture will be of a lightly tinted, creamy consistency) and marinate for 1 hour.

3. Put ½ cup of the mixture into the center of each foil square. Fold over to the center from each side and tuck the two ends under to form a 4-inch square.

4. Steam in a Chinese-style steamer over moderate heat for 1 hour. Unfold the packets and serve at room temperature.

MAKES 11 TO 12 PACKETS

WETTHA HTAMIN HTOKE
Pork and Rice Package

This recipe originates in Taunggyi, the Shan State capital, where they wrap the packages in banana leaves before steaming them. Since banana leaves are now available here in Oriental shops, it is recommended that you try to locate some and use them to add a fresh green flavor.

2 cups cooked warm rice
½ pound ground pork, about 1 cup
2 tablespoons light soy sauce
1 teaspoon salt

Banana leaves (optional)

Aluminum foil, cut into 10-inch squares
1 tablespoon Crispy Fried Onions (see Index)
1 teaspoon Crispy Garlic Slices (see Index)
4 scallions, sliced

1. Mix the warm rice, pork, soy sauce, and salt together.

2. Put a 6-inch strip of banana leaf on each foil square. In the center put one quarter of the pork and rice mixture. Fold the leaf and sheet into an oblong roll about 5 inches long and 2 inches in diameter. Press the mixture down tightly and seal the ends of the foil roll by twisting. Prepare 4 packages in this fashion.

3. Steam the packages in a Chinese-style steamer over moderate heat for 1 hour.

4. Unfold, and garnish the roll with onion, garlic, and scallion.

Serve warm as a snack with tea, coffee, or drinks.

SERVES 4

Variation: The packages may be prepared as a single loaf and served in slices. Press the rice/pork mixture firmly into an 8-inch heatproof glass baking dish. Cover the loaf with a square of banana leaf and cover the dish tightly with aluminum foil. Steam in a Chinese-style steamer over moderate heat for 1 hour.

WETTHA PAUNG

Colonial Pork Loaf

This is an Anglo-Burmese dish from a community that had both English and Burmese blood. It is a recipe from the Colonial period in Burma and clearly reflects English tastes. Compared to this Burmese recipe, the vividly spiced Anglo-Indian food is much closer to Indian taste than to English.

2 pounds pork, ground
3 garlic cloves, chopped fine
2 medium-size onions, chopped, 1 cup
2 teaspoons salt
¼ teaspoon ground pepper
4 eggs, beaten

1. Mix the pork with the garlic, onion, salt, pepper, and 1 egg.

2. Put the mixture into an 8-inch heatproof glass dish. Pour 3 eggs over the surface of the loaf so that eggs completely cover the meat.

3. Steam in a Chinese-style steamer for 45 minutes. The eggs will rise like a soufflé, while the bottom of the loaf produces a clear, strong broth, which is the sauce.

Serve warm in slices.

SERVES 6 TO 8

WETTHA BAUNG

Burmese Pork Loaf

This version of the pork loaf is more intensely flavored than the Colonial Pork Loaf. Garlic especially is heavy; you may wish to reduce the quantity somewhat. The original Burmese recipe used 2 tablespoons of chopped garlic!

1 pound pork, ground
1 medium-size onion, chopped, ½ cup
1 tablespoon fine-chopped garlic
1 egg, beaten
2 teaspoons rice flour
¼ teaspoon salt
1 teaspoon sugar
2 teaspoons soy sauce

1. Thoroughly mix all ingredients together and turn the mixture into a shallow flameproof dish so that the loaf is about 2 inches high.

2. Steam in a Chinese-style steamer over water over moderate heat for 45 minutes.

Serve warm with a sauce of your choice such as Worcestershire, sweet soy sauce, hot chili sauce.

SERVES 4

Variation: Ground beef is an excellent and popular substitute for the pork. Use the same ingredients, but steam for only 30 minutes.

WET NANYO KYAW

Fried Spareribs with Star Anise

This is a Sino-Burmese specialty from Maymyo, a hillside town named for Colonel May of the British Army. An attractive town in the cool hills, it was a retreat from the bone-melting heat of the plains, during the British Colonial period. These ribs make an admirable appetizer with drinks. Each morsel is exotically seasoned with the star anise and nicely managed with your fingers. On the other hand, if preferred, the ribs may be included in a variety of dishes for lunch or dinner.

> *2 pounds meaty pork spareribs, cut into 1-inch cubes*
> *1 egg yolk*
> *1 teaspoon salt*
> *Oil for deep-frying, about 2 cups*
> *1 teaspoon ground star anise*
> *1 cup thin-sliced leeks, both white and tender green parts*
> *1 tablespoon soy sauce*

1. Marinate the pork in the egg yolk and salt for 1 to 2 hours.

2. In a wok or skillet heat the oil over moderate heat for 5 minutes. Cool the oil to room temperature (an important step).

3. Add the spareribs, one by one, to the oil, and fry them over moderate heat for 30 minutes, or until brown. Stir once or twice during this process. Remove the ribs and drain them in a metal sieve. Set aside.

4. Remove all the oil except 1 tablespoon. Add the star anise and the leeks and stir-fry over moderate heat for 1 minute. Add the soy sauce, stir a moment, then return the ribs to the pan and stir-fry for 1 minute more.

Serve warm as a main dish with other foods.

SERVES 6

WETSHE THOAT
Braised, Caramelized Tongue

This preparation has a faintly sweet citrus flavor that is unconventional. It is considered a side dish and is best served with bread or rolls.

TONGUE
1 pork tongue, 1 to 1½ pounds
1 tablespoon corn or peanut oil
2 teaspoons brown sugar
1 garlic clove, chopped
2 teaspoons soy sauce
1 teaspoon salt
1 cup water

SAUCE
1 tablespoon lime juice
1 teaspoon brown sugar
1 teaspoon soy sauce
1 teaspoon thin-sliced fresh hot green chili
1 tablespoon chopped fresh coriander leaves

1. Scrape the tongue firmly with a serrated or sharp knife to remove as much of the skin as you can without cutting. Rinse.

2. Heat the oil in a pan, add the sugar, and stir over moderate heat for 1 minute, or until sugar melts. Add the garlic and stir-fry for another minute. The color will become quite dark.

3. Add the tongue and brown it all over in the caramelized sauce for about 2 minutes. Add the soy sauce and salt and continue to brown for 2 minutes as the sauce reduces to a hiss in the pan.

4. Add the water and bring to a boil. Cover the pan and cook over moderately low heat for 1 hour, or until the tongue is tender and the sauce has reduced to about 3 tablespoons.

5. Remove tongue to a cutting board and cut it diagonally into slices about ¼ inch thick. Return slices to the pan and coat them with the sauce. Keep warm.

(continued on next page)

6. Mix the lime juice, sugar, soy sauce, and chili together to make a sauce.

7. Place tongue slices on a serving platter, pour the lime sauce over them, and sprinkle with chopped coriander.

Serve warm.

SERVES 4

Variation: A veal tongue weighing about 2 pounds produces an exceptionally flavorful dish. The tongue must be boiled in water in a covered pan over moderate heat for 30 minutes to loosen the skin. Drain and pull off the tongue skin. Continue the steps as for the pork tongue, but double the amount of ingredients.

WET KALAZA HIN

Curried Pork Innards

This is an extraordinary Burmese-style curry, with the different meats providing different textures and flavors. Chinese or other Asian butcher shops will have the innards for sale, all cleaned. Prepared mango pickle of either hot or medium (chili) intensity may be purchased in most Asian food shops.

PORK

½ pound liver, cut into 2-inch-wide slices
1 pancreas, cut into 2-inch-wide slices (optional)
1 small heart, halved, trimmed, cut into 2-inch-wide slices
½ pound stomach, cut into 2-inch-wide slices
½ pound boneless meat, cut into 1-inch cubes

2 teaspoons salt
2 tablespoons soy sauce
2 tablespoons prepared mango pickle, medium-hot
2 tablespoons corn or peanut oil
½ teaspoon ground turmeric

2 medium-size onions, chopped, 1 cup
1 tablespoon fine-chopped fresh ginger
4 garlic cloves, chopped fine, 1 tablespoon
2 teaspoons ground cuminseed, lightly toasted in dry skillet
½ teaspoon star anise, seeds or ground
4 cups pork broth or water

1. Soak the liver in cold water for 30 minutes. Drain and set aside.

2. Marinate together the pancreas, heart, stomach, and boneless pork with 1 teaspoon salt, 1 tablespoon soy sauce, and the mango pickle for 15 minutes.

3. Heat a large pan for a moment, then add the oil and turmeric. Stir-fry the onions, ginger, and garlic over moderate heat until brown, about 3 minutes. Add the cuminseed and anise during this time.

4. Add the marinated meats and stir well to brown them for 2 minutes. Cover the pan and cook for 15 minutes to prepare a well-browned sauce.

5. Add the liver, remaining 1 teaspoon salt, remaining 1 tablespoon soy sauce, and the broth or water. Cook the curry over moderately low heat for 1 hour, or until the meats are tender. The sauce will have reduced by half and thickened.

Serve warm with rice and other dishes, with Indian breads, or pita-style bread, known in Burma as *nampya*.

SERVES 4 TO 6

Variation: Beef innards, cut into 2-inch pieces, may also be utilized for a curry, using the same ingredients as for the pork. The recipe will be adequate for 3 pounds of beef innards. Cooking time and technique of preparation will be the same.

SHAN WET OO CHANG

Shan-Style Sausages

I have eaten and cooked this sausage, a specialty of the Shan people, when visiting in their capital, Taunggyi, a mountain resort in the section of Burma bordered by China, Laos, and Thailand. It is homemade and prepared with natural ingredients only—no artificial coloring, MSG, chemicals to extend shelf life, or other abominations of the industrial age. It is easy to prepare and becomes easier with experience. Pork casings may be purchased in ethnic (such as Italian) meat markets. In Burma, the Shan people generally use the small intestines of sheep as casing since they are more tender. Because sheep casings are not as large in diameter, there would be more sausages.

2 pounds boneless pork shoulder, cut into ¼-inch pieces
2 garlic cloves, chopped fine
1 inch of fresh ginger, chopped fine
1 teaspoon dried hot red chili flakes
⅛ teaspoon ground turmeric
1 teaspoon salt
2 teaspoons sugar
1 tablespoon dark soy sauce
1 tablespoon rice wine or dry sherry
1 pork sausage casing (weighs about 4 ounces)

1. Mix together everything except the casing. Cover the dish and refrigerate overnight.

2. Fit a funnel with a ½-inch opening into the end of the casing. Pull about 6 inches of the casing up over the funnel opening.

3. Push the pork through the opening into the casing with a chopstick or similar utensil. Fill the entire casing. Tie both ends closed with a thread. Cut off any casing that is not filled.

4. To divide into sausages, pinch the casing about 4 inches from the end, squeezing the pork aside so that you can twist the casing around three times. Prepare all the sausages this way, pushing and twisting. Tie each sausage off with a string.

5. In a dry skillet, over moderate heat, fry the sausages for 1 minute, turning them over once. Poke several holes in the air pockets of each sausage with a needle to allow the air to escape.

6. Remove the sausages, which are still attached in a long string, and steam them in a Chinese-style steamer over moderate heat for 30 minutes. At this stage the sausage may be refrigerated for up to 2 weeks.

7. When ready to use, cut each sausage off at the place it was tied. Brown them in 1 tablespoon oil in a skillet over moderate heat for about 5 minutes.

Serve warm with rice and bread.

MAKES 5 OR 6 SAUSAGES, EACH 4 INCHES LONG AND 1 INCH IN DIAMETER

WETTHA HMYIT CHIN

Bacon with Sour Bamboo Shoots

This pork dish can be adapted to one's personal taste. When prepared as given here, it is a thick stew in the style of the Pa-O tribe of the Shan State. When prepared with considerably more water, resulting in a soupy consistency, it is in the style prepared elsewhere throughout Burma. I prefer the Pa-O method, but you can judge for yourself.

2 pounds fresh slab bacon, with skin, fat, and meat, cut into 2-inch cubes
1 can (1 pound, 3 ounces) sour bamboo shoots, drained and sliced thin
2 tablespoons chopped onion
1 large garlic clove, chopped
½ teaspoon chopped fresh ginger
1 teaspoon salt
3 teaspoons fish sauce
⅛ teaspoon ground turmeric
1 teaspoon corn or peanut oil
3 cups water

1. Mix everything except the water together in a pan. Stir-fry over moderately high heat for 8 minutes or so. This will lightly brown the bacon.

2. Add the water, bring to a boil, and cook, covered, over moderately low heat for about 1½ hours. This will reduce the liquid by half and tenderize the pork.

Serve warm with rice and other dishes. This tastes better the second day when briefly rewarmed.

SERVES 6

POULTRY AND EGGS

Chickens in Burma are treated with a great deal of respect for their potential culinary future. There you will not find simple, little recipes with timid seasonings, but rather pungent spices that glorify the richly flavorful village chickens. Burma is not industrialized, therefore whatever poultry is raised is done so with the uncontaminated fresh feed and greens of the rural countryside.

Chicken is prepared with well-seasoned sauces of many variations, colored with turmeric and paprika, often bathed in coconut milk and surrounded with assorted vegetables. The hot chili pleasantly surprises the palate and fish sauce *(nam pya yi)* continues in its indispensable role.

I tend to use the fresh Cornish game hen of the American supermarket since it closely resembles in flavor, texture, and size the Burmese village chicken. When preparing the chicken recipes, I suggest you try the game hen since it is interchangeable in these dishes with an equal weight in chicken.

Ducks, too, are prepared in imaginative ways but within the traditional framework. Wherever there are rivers, lakes, ample rainfall, and unlimited grazing greens, one will find the Burmese duck in large numbers.

KYETTHA SABAUNG
Salt-Baked Cornish Game Hen

1 Cornish game hen, 1½ to 2 pounds, halved
¼ teaspoon ground turmeric
¼ teaspoon salt
2 pounds coarse (kosher) salt
Aluminum foil
3 sheets of typing paper

1. Rub both halves of the hen inside and out with the turmeric and salt. Set aside.

2. Select a heavy pan with a cover, just a little larger than the hen. Half-fill the pan with coarse salt. Wrap the hen in a single layer of foil and seal the package well so that the juices do not run out into the salt. Place the package over the salt and cover it completely with more salt, almost up to the top of the pan.

3. Trace around the cover of the pan on each sheet of paper and cut out the forms. Soak each sheet in water and place it over the salt. Cover the pan tightly.

4. Put the pan on the top of the stove, gas or electric, and "bake" over moderate heat for 30 minutes. The paper cutouts will have dried out, which indicates that the hen is cooked. Let the pan stand off the heating element for another 30 minutes to cool off.

To serve, remove the foil package from the salt. Unfold, and serve the hen as an appetizer with drinks or with other dishes in a meal.

SERVES 4

Note: Salt is the cooking medium and does not influence the taste since the foil package is (or should be) well sealed. The salt may be used again to bake another hen or for other purposes.

KYET ROAST

Chicken Roast

This is an Anglo-Burmese type of preparation, dating from the Colonial period.

1 tablespoon butter
2 tablespoons corn or peanut oil
1 garlic clove, chopped
1 chicken, 3 pounds, quartered, or 2 Cornish game hens, halved
1 teaspoon salt
6 peppercorns
3 bay leaves
½ pound cauliflower, cut into 2-inch florets
12 green snap beans, whole
2 small carrots, halved
½ cup water
Oil for frying potatoes
3 medium-size potatoes, peeled and halved, parboiled for 10
    minutes

1. Melt the butter and oil together in a pan. Brown the garlic and chicken over moderate heat for 10 minutes.

2. Add the salt, peppercorns, bay leaves, cauliflower, green beans, carrots, and water. Cover the pan and cook for 20 minutes more, or until chicken and vegetables are tender.

3. Heat oil in a skillet and brown-crisp the potatoes for about 10 minutes. Serve potatoes as a garnish with the chicken.

Serve warm.

SERVES 4

KYET KALAE ASA THUT

Stuffed Cornish Game Hen

STUFFING

> 1 tablespoon corn or peanut oil
> ¼ cup ¼-inch carrot dice
> ¼ cup ¼-inch pumpkin or butternut squash dice
> ½ cup shredded potato
> 2 tablespoons chopped onion
> 1 teaspoon chopped fresh ginger
> 1 garlic clove, chopped
> 1 tablespoon soy sauce
> ½ teaspoon salt
> 1 tablespoon water
> 4 shelled quail eggs (canned), (optional)

HEN

> 1 Cornish game hen, about 1½ pounds
> 1 teaspoon soy sauce
> ½ teaspoon salt
> 1 tablespoon corn or peanut oil
> 3 teaspoons brown or white sugar
> ½ teaspoon pepper
> 1 cup water

1. To make the stuffing, heat the oil in a skillet and over moderate heat stir-fry the rest of the stuffing ingredients except the water and the quail eggs for 2 minutes. Add the water and stir-fry for 1 minute more. Set aside.

2. Rub the hen inside and out with the soy sauce and salt. Stuff the hen with the stuffing and the quail eggs. Sew it up.

3. Heat the oil in a pan, add the sugar, and let it caramelize over moderate heat for 1 to 2 minutes. Add the pepper and the hen. Brown the hen in the caramelized oil for 3 to 4 minutes.

4. Add the water, cover the pan, and cook for 40 minutes, turning the hen several times to brown it completely to a golden brown color. Just before serving, sprinkle the top of the hen with a few pinches of pepper.

Serve warm.

SERVES 2 GENEROUSLY

Note: Quail eggs can be purchased canned in Asian food stores and in some supermarkets. On the other hand you might be able to find fresh quail eggs; if so, hard-cook them and add to the stuffing.

MALAY KYAUK SWE

Malay Noodle Stir-Fry

This is a Sino-Burmese recipe that has been influenced equally by each culture.

> *1 tablespoon corn or peanut oil*
> *2 garlic cloves, sliced thin*
> *½ inch of fresh ginger, chopped fine*
> *1 tablespoon sliced onion*
> *1 teaspoon dried hot red chili flakes*
> *½ pound boneless chicken, cut into ½-inch cubes, about 1 cup*
> *1 tablespoon soy sauce*
> *½ teaspoon salt*
> *2 cups shredded cabbage*
> *1 fresh rice sheet, cut into ½-inch-wide strips 3 inches long*
> *¼ cup chopped celery leaves*

1. Heat the oil in a wok and fry the garlic and ginger over moderate heat for 2 minutes. Add the onion and chili and stir-fry for 1 minute.

2. Add the chicken and stir-fry until the color changes. Add the soy sauce, salt, and cabbage, and stir-fry for 2 minutes. Add the rice sheet strips and stir-fry for 3 minutes to mix well.

3. Add the celery leaves, mix, and serve.

Serve warm.

SERVES 4

ON NO KYAUK SWE

Chicken Curry with Coconut Milk Gravy and Garnishes

Kyauk swe (pronounced COW-sway) is probably the best known of all Burmese dishes—well known in Asia, that is, but unfortunately not elsewhere. Old Burmese hands from the Colonial period will remember it well and with considerable nostalgia. It is a preparation easily adapted to the American kitchen, as a one-dish meal for parties large and small. The list of ingredients is not extensive and they are all available in Asian markets. Coconut milk may be prepared at home, but a fine quality milk from Thailand is available, and it is a great timesaver.

CURRY

> 1 chicken, 3½ pounds, or 1 pound boneless chicken, both light and
>   dark meat
> 3 tablespoons corn or peanut oil
> ½ cup chopped onion
> 1 inch of fresh ginger, chopped
> 4 garlic cloves, chopped
> ½ teaspoon ground turmeric
> 2 teaspoons paprika
> 3 tablespoons fish sauce
> 1 teaspoon salt

GRAVY

> 10 cups homemade chicken broth
> 1½ cups chick-pea flour (besan), soaked in 2 cups water for 30
>   minutes
> ½ pound shallots, peeled
> 2 cups rich Coconut Milk (see Index)
> 1 tablespoon fish sauce

GARNISHES

> 2 pounds fresh egg noodles, cooked and drained according to
>   directions
> 1 cup onion slices, rinsed under cold water, drained
> 6 hard-cooked eggs
> 2 cups (½ pound) crispy fried noodles, purchased or homemade

1 cup chopped fresh coriander
Dried hot red chili flakes, lightly toasted in a dry skillet
Lemon wedges

1. Divide the chicken into convenient pieces; remove and discard loose skin and fat. Bone the chicken: remove the meat from all parts except the back, which may be used for another purpose. Cut the meat into ½-inch cubes.

2. Heat the oil in a large pan. Fry the onion, ginger, and garlic over moderate heat for 2 minutes. Add the turmeric and paprika and continue to stir-fry.

3. Add the chicken, fish sauce, and salt. Stir-fry the mixture for 10 minutes.

4. To make the gravy, add the broth to the pan of curry, and bring to a boil over moderate heat. Add the chick-pea *(besan)* liquid and cook for 20 minutes, stirring continuously since the *besan* has a tendency to stick. The gravy will begin to thicken.

5. Add the shallots as the gravy simmers, and cook for 10 minutes. Now add the coconut milk and fish sauce and cook for 10 minutes more, stirring constantly.

6. For each serving, fill soup bowls with the ingredients in this order:

½ cup cooked egg noodles
1 tablespoon onion slices
hard-cooked egg slices
1 cup hot chicken curry with gravy
2 tablespoons crispy noodles
2 teaspoons fresh coriander
hot chili flakes, to taste
lemon wedges, to squeeze over all

For the second helping, each diner simply adds what pleases him most.

SERVES 10 TO 12

Note: An optional but popular garnish is the Chicken Liver Appetizer (Athe Amyit Hin, see Index). If this is used, it should be added as the last thing.

SHWE DAUNG KYAUK SWE

Chicken Curry Shwe Daung Style

Shwe Daung (Gold Mountain) is a town in Middle Burma that features this noodle and chicken dish. It is a simpler version of the On No Kyauk Swe and a good introduction to this famous Burmese dish.

1 pound fresh egg noodles, cooked and drained according to package directions
1 cup onion slices, rinsed under cold water, drained
1 recipe Chicken Curry (On No Kyauk Swe, see Index)
1 cup fresh rich Coconut Milk (see Index)
2 cups crispy fried noodles, purchased (½ pound)
1 cup chopped fresh coriander
Lemon wedges

Serve in soup bowls in the following order:

½ cup egg noodles
1 tablespoon onion
½ cup or more warm chicken curry
2 tablespoons coconut milk sprinkled over all
1 tablespoon crispy noodles
1 tablespoon coriander
Lemon juice to taste

For the second helping each diner will add the quantity and variety according to personal preference.

SERVES 6

KYET THA SIPYAN

Chicken Curry

This standard Burmese curry is eaten all over the country. Browning the chicken before the water is added is vital to the color and aroma of the curry and also to preparing the thick sauce. This same method is used in many of their meat recipes.

> 1 chicken, 3½ pounds, cut into 8 serving pieces, loose skin and fat discarded
> 1 teaspoon salt
> ½ teaspoon ground turmeric
> 4 tablespoons fish sauce
> 2 small onions, sliced, ½ cup
> 4 garlic cloves, sliced
> 1 inch of fresh ginger, sliced
> 1 teaspoon paprika
> 1 teaspoon dried hot red chili flakes, moistened in 2 teaspoons water
> 3 tablespoons corn or peanut oil
> ¼ cup chopped ripe tomato
> ½ cup water

1. Mix the chicken with the salt, turmeric, and fish sauce and marinate for 15 minutes.

2. Pound in a mortar or process together to a coarse paste the onions, garlic, ginger, paprika, and chili flakes.

3. Heat the oil in a pan, add the ground ingredients, and stir-fry over moderate heat until light brown. Add the chicken and tomato and stir-fry for about 15 minutes. You will notice that the oil separates or rises in the mixture.

4. Add the water, cover the pan, and cook over moderately low heat for about 25 minutes, until the chicken is tender and the sauce reduced to a thick consistency.

Serve warm.

SERVES 4

PANTHE KYAUK SWE

Egg Noodles, Chinese Muslim Style

This is a special noodle dish prepared by the Panthe, who are Chinese Muslims resident in Burma. It is usually sold by traveling hawkers but also in some Muslim restaurants. It is seldom prepared in the home.

CHICKEN CURRY

>1 pound boneless chicken, light or dark meat, cut into 1-inch cubes
>¼ teaspoon ground turmeric
>1 teaspoon paprika
>1 teaspoon ground cuminseed
>½ teaspoon salt
>2 teaspoons soy sauce
>2 tablespoons corn or peanut oil
>1 cup sliced onion
>1 garlic clove, chopped
>½ pound ripe tomatoes, sliced
>½ cup chicken broth

NOODLES

>1 pound egg noodles, number 9 spaghetti size
>1 tablespoon corn or peanut oil
>1 tablespoon soy sauce

GARNISHES

>2 scallions, sliced
>½ cup shredded cabbage
>Lemon or lime juice
>½ to 1 teaspoon roasted dried hot red chili flakes

1. Marinate the chicken for 15 minutes with the turmeric, paprika, cuminseed, salt, and soy sauce.

2. Heat the oil in a pan, add the onion and garlic, and stir-fry over moderate heat for 2 minutes. Add the tomatoes and fry for 1 minute. Add the chicken and stir-fry for 2 minutes.

3. Add the chicken broth, mix well, and cover the pan. Cook for 20 minutes. Set aside and keep warm.

4. Cook the noodles in boiling water for 3 minutes. Rinse under cold water and drain well. Mix the noodles, oil, and soy sauce together. Set aside.

5. Put the noodles in a large serving platter. Pour the entire curry over the noodles. Garnish with the scallion slices, cabbage, and lemon or lime juice and chili flakes to taste.

Serve warm or at room temperature.

SERVES 4 TO 6

Note: To roast the chili flakes, put 2 tablespoons flakes in a dry skillet. Toast them over moderately low heat for 2 minutes, or until the color darkens and the aroma (very pungent) is released. Shake the skillet frequently during this process.

YINMABIN-CHOWLE KYATTHA

Mr. Soley's Chicken Curry

It took us three years to obtain this recipe. This is how it happened. My coauthor and his students from the University of Rangoon were involved in a literacy campaign in Pindaya township during 1967-1970. They would always pass a certain small restaurant in their travels and the students would order this particular chicken curry. It was so outstanding that they kept asking for the recipe, but the owner, a Burmese of Indian origin, whose name was Soley (pronounced CHOW-LEE in Burmese) always refused. He guarded his famous recipe since it was upon this that the reputation of his restaurant was based; it was his principal means of earning a living.

We had no luck trying to reproduce the taste or technique at home no matter how many times we ordered and ate the curry. After three years and innumerable servings of chicken, my friend once more asked Soley for the recipe in view of the long friendship and considerable investment that they had made in the restaurant. He consented at last and so we are able to include it in this book.

CHICKEN

1 chicken, 3 pounds, quartered
½ teaspoon ground turmeric
2 teaspoons salt
2 tablespoons corn or peanut oil
1 tablespoon brown sugar
5 peppercorns, cracked

SPICES

1 tablespoon coriander seeds
1 tablespoon white poppy seeds
½ teaspoon fenugreek seeds
½ teaspoon black mustard seeds
1 tablespoon whole cuminseeds
4 cardamom pods
½ teaspoon star anise, 3 or 4 lobes
½ cup water

CURRY GRAVY
> *1 medium-size onion, sliced, ½ cup*
> *3 large garlic cloves, sliced*
> *1 inch of fresh ginger, sliced*
> *1 teaspoon paprika*
> *2 tablespoons corn or peanut oil*
> *⅛ teaspoon ground turmeric*
> *½ cup plain yogurt*

1. Rub the chicken with the turmeric and salt and let stand for 15 minutes.

2. Heat the oil in a pan over moderate heat and add the sugar, stirring until it melts. Add the peppercorns and chicken pieces. Brown the chicken on all sides for 10 minutes. Remove chicken and set aside.

3. Mix the spices together and toast them in a dry skillet over moderately low heat for 2 minutes. Stir continuously.

4. Blend spices into a powder, mix with the water, and set aside.

5. To make the gravy, put the onion, garlic, ginger, and paprika into a processor and chop fine.

6. Heat the oil in a pan and over moderate heat fry the onion/garlic mixture and the turmeric until light brown. Add the spices and water, mix, and stir well for 2 minutes to release the aroma. Add the yogurt and stir-fry for 2 minutes.

7. Add the chicken pieces, cover the pan, and cook over moderately low heat for 30 minutes. This should be enough time to tenderize the chicken and reduce the sauce.

Serve warm with rice and other dishes.

SERVES 4

Variation: Either lamb or beef may be substituted for the chicken. Cut 2 pounds meat into 2-inch cubes. Use the same ingredients as for a 3-pound chicken except the water should be doubled and the cooking time extended to 1 hour, or a bit more, to tenderize the meat.

KALA THA CHET

Bachelor's Chicken

This is known as "bachelor's chicken" after the Burmese young men, who, it is related, wander out at midnight on moonless nights looking for excitement. They like to steal a chicken and cook it over a wood fire in a clandestine fashion. This preparation is midway between a soup and a curry; it has a considerable amount of liquid, and turns a pleasant red color from the paprika.

> 1 chicken, 3½ pounds cut into 10 serving pieces, including giblets;
>   loose skin and fat discarded
> 2 stalks of lemongrass, cut into 3 pieces each, slightly crushed
> 1 medium-size onion, sliced, ½ cup
> 3 garlic cloves, crushed to a paste
> 1 inch of fresh ginger, crushed to a paste
> 1 teaspoon paprika
> 1 teaspoon dried hot red chili flakes
> ¼ teaspoon ground turmeric
> 1 teaspoon salt
> 3 tablespoons fish sauce
> 2 tablespoons corn or peanut oil
> 5 cups water

1. Put everything into a pan except the water. Stir-fry over moderate heat for about 15 minutes, until the mixture is lightly browned.

2. Add the water, bring to a boil, and cook over moderate heat for about 30 minutes, until the chicken is tender.

Serve warm.

SERVES 6

KYETTHA SIKYAN YAKYAN

Spiced Game Hen Stew

A literal translation of the title tells us that water and oil are cooked together with the hen so that a substantial amount of sauce remains —the water remains, the oil remains—but the dish is not soupy. All that in three Burmese words.

1 tablespoon corn or peanut oil
⅛ teaspoon ground turmeric
2 tablespoons thin-sliced onion
½ teaspoon chopped fresh ginger
1 garlic clove, sliced
½ teaspoon dried hot red chili flakes
1 stalk of lemongrass, cut into 4-inch pieces and lightly pounded
1 Cornish game hen, including giblets, cut into 8 pieces
1 tablespoon fish sauce
½ teaspoon salt
1 cup chicken broth

1. Heat the oil in a pan and add the turmeric, onion, ginger, garlic, and chili flakes, and stir-fry over moderate heat for 2 minutes. Add the lemongrass and fry for 1 minute more.

2. Add the hen and fry for 4 minutes, stirring constantly.

3. Add the fish sauce, salt, and broth. Bring to a boil, cover the pan, and cook over moderately low heat for 30 minutes. The sauce will reduce and thicken.

Serve warm with rice and salad.

SERVES 4

KYETTHA KALAPE HIN

Chicken and Chick-Pea Curry

1 chicken, 3 pounds, cut into 8 to 10 serving pieces, loose skin and
    fat discarded
2 tablespoons chopped onion
2 garlic cloves, chopped
½ inch of fresh ginger, chopped
½ teaspoon ground turmeric
1 teaspoon paprika
1 teaspoon dried hot red chili flakes
1 teaspoon salt
2 teaspoons ground cuminseed
2 tablespoons corn or peanut oil
2 cups water
1 can (1 pound) chick-peas, drained well and half crushed

1. Mix all ingredients except water and chick-peas together in a
pan and marinate for 15 minutes.

2. Cook the mixture over moderate heat for 5 minutes. Add 1 cup
water and continue to cook, covered, for 20 minutes.

3. Add the chick-peas and cook for 10 minutes longer to develop
a thick sauce. Add the balance of the water, uncover the pan, and
simmer over low heat for 15 minutes more.

Serve warm with rice.

SERVES 6

Note: I am suggesting canned, cooked chick-peas since they are
perfectly adequate to incorporate in the curry. Half-crushing the peas
with a fork mashes some of them to make a thickening agent for this
curry, a method both unusual and flavorful.

BUTHI-KYETTHA HIN

Chicken and Long Gourd Curry

This curry is a favorite in Burma partly because of the great popularity of the long gourd throughout the country. A proverb says: "You only come to see me and call me 'uncle' when the long gourd is ready to eat."

1 chicken, 3½ pounds, or 2 Cornish game hens
2 pounds long gourd
2 tablespoons fish sauce
½ teaspoon ground turmeric
1 teaspoon paprika
1 medium-size onion, crushed to a paste, ½ cup
1 inch of fresh ginger, crushed to a paste
2 garlic cloves, crushed to a paste
1 teaspoon salt
2 tablespoons corn or peanut oil
1 stalk of lemongrass, halved, lightly cracked to release the flavor
1 cup water

1. Cut the chicken into 10 serving pieces. Discard loose skin and fat.

2. Peel the long gourd and cut it into ¼-inch-thick slices.

3. Mix all other ingredients except water in a pan, and add the chicken and gourd. Cover the pan and cook over moderate heat for 10 minutes.

4. Add the water, bring to a boil, and continue to cook for another 20 minutes, until the chicken is tender. There should be sufficient sauce since the gourd is a watery vegetable.

Serve warm with rice and other dishes.

MAKES 4 TO 6 SERVINGS

DAN BAUK

Spiced Chicken and Rice

The Burmese, always on the lookout for culinary excitement, were quick to adopt the Indian rice and lamb dish, *biryani*, and make it their own. Prepared with chicken and called *dan bauk*, this Indo-Burmese concoction has become the most-requested dish at catered weddings and other celebrations in Rangoon. The food shops and small restaurants in the center of town attract hungry diners by featuring enormous caldrons of this chicken and rice combination. They have taken to it like the proverbial duck to water.

CHICKEN

> 2 teaspoons salt
> ⅛ teaspoon ground turmeric
> 1 chicken, 3½ pounds, cut into 8 pieces
> ¼ cup corn or peanut oil

RICE

> 8 cardamom pods
> ¼ teaspoon ground turmeric
> 2 teaspoons paprika
> 1 tablespoon garam masala
> 1 teaspoon ground cuminseed
> 1 cinnamon stick, 3 inches long
> 1 teaspoon salt
> 4 cups raw rice
> 5 cups water or homemade chicken broth
> 1 cup Crispy Fried Onions (see Index)
> 2 cups dairy sour cream
> 1 cup fresh or frozen green peas
> ½ cup dark raisins
> 1 teaspoon whole saffron, soaked in 2 tablespoons warm water
>   (optional)

1. Mix salt and turmeric together, rub into chicken, and let stand for 15 minutes.

2. Heat the oil in a skillet and brown the chicken on both sides over moderate heat for 5 minutes. Remove chicken and set aside.

3. Heat the same oil in a large pan and add to it the cardamom, turmeric, paprika, *garam masala*, cuminseed, cinnamon, and salt. Stir-fry for 1 minute, add the rice, and stir-fry over moderate heat for 2 minutes more.

4. Add the water or broth, bring to a boil, and cover the pan. Reduce heat to low and simmer for 7 minutes to half-cook the rice.

5. Add the chicken, crispy onions, sour cream, green peas, raisins, and saffron if used. Mix everything together, cover the pan, and cook slowly over low heat for 30 to 40 minutes. Do not stir the mixture during this time but shake the pan back and forth several times so sauce will not stick to pan.

Dan bauk can also be baked in the oven rather than on top of the stove. When all the ingredients are mixed together, cover the pan and bake in a 325°F. oven for 30 to 40 minutes.

Serve chicken and rice warm with a light soup and with the Dan Bauk Salad (see Index).

SERVES 8

Variation: Cornish game hens are also good in this recipe. Cut each one into 4 pieces.

KYET TAUNG-PAN RAKHINE-CHET

Chicken Wing Curry

6 full chicken wings
½ teaspoon ground turmeric
½ teaspoon salt
1 medium-size onion, sliced, ½ cup
1 large garlic clove, sliced
½ inch piece of fresh ginger, sliced
1 semihot green chili, sliced
2 tablespoons corn or peanut oil
2 teaspoons shrimp paste
1 cup water

1. Cut off and discard the wing tips. Divide the other wing sections at the joint. Marinate the wings with turmeric and salt for 10 minutes.

2. Process The onion, garlic, ginger, and chili together to a coarse paste. Heat the oil in a pan and stir-fry the onion mixture and shrimp paste over moderate heat for 2 minutes. Add the wings and brown for 3 minutes more.

3. Add the water, cover the pan, and cook for 30 minutes, until the wings are tender and the sauce reduced to a thick consistency.

Serve warm with rice or bread and other dishes.

SERVES 4 TO 6

Variation: A small broiler chicken or Cornish game hen, cut into 8 pieces, may be used instead of the chicken wings. Use the same recipe for 2 pounds of poultry.

KYET KIN

Barbecued Chicken

The marinade has an unusual flavor largely because of the fermented tofu. This may be purchased in Asian groceries in jars, cubed, fermented, and packed with small flakes of dried hot red chili. I serve cubes of the leftover *si tofu* with toothpicks to accompany drinks.

> 1 chicken, 3 pounds, or 2 Cornish game hens
> 1 cube of si tofu (fermented tofu)
> 2 teaspoons honey
> 1 tablespoon lime juice
> 2 tablespoons soy sauce
> 1 teaspoon shrimp paste
> 1 teaspoon paprika
> 2 teaspoons corn or peanut oil

1. Cut the chicken or game hens into quarters. Discard loose skin and fat.

2. Mash the tofu and mix it with the honey, lime juice, soy sauce, shrimp paste, paprika, and oil to prepare a marinade.

3. Rub the chicken pieces with the marinade and let stand for not less than 1 hour, longer is better.

4. Broil in a gas or electric oven for about 6 minutes on each side. It is even better barbecued over charcoal.

Serve warm.

SERVES 4

KYETTHA ASEIN KYAW

Chicken Fry with Vegetables

1 cup ½-inch cubes of boneless chicken or Cornish game hen
4 teaspoons soy sauce
4 teaspoons fish sauce
1 tablespoon corn or peanut oil
½ inch of fresh ginger, chopped
1 garlic clove, chopped
½ cup thin-sliced carrots
½ cup snow peas, strung
1 cup ¼-inch slices of Chinese cabbage
½ cup cauliflower florets
½ cup water
½ teaspoon salt

1. Marinate the chicken with 2 teaspoons each of soy sauce and fish sauce for 15 minutes.

2. Heat the oil in a wok or skillet and stir-fry ginger and garlic over moderate heat for 1 minute. Add the chicken and stir-fry until the color changes, about 2 minutes.

3. Add the carrots, snow peas, cabbage, and cauliflower, and stir-fry for 2 minutes, adding the balance of the soy and fish sauce. Add water and salt and stir-fry for 5 minutes.

4. Cover the wok, remove it from heat, and let it stand for 5 minutes to steam through.

Serve warm with other dishes.

SERVES 4

KYETTHA KONBONGYI

Chili Chicken

1 small chicken breast, cut into ½-inch pieces, about 1 cup
1 egg, separated
⅛ teaspoon salt
1 tablespoon corn or peanut oil
1 small garlic clove, chopped fine
½ teaspoon chopped fresh ginger
2 tablespoons chopped onion
1 tablespoon sliced fresh semihot green chili
1 teaspoon soy sauce
1 scallion, cut into ½-inch pieces
1 tablespoon chopped fresh coriander

1. Mix the chicken, egg yolk, and salt together and let stand for 5 minutes.

2. Heat the oil in a skillet and over high heat fry the garlic and ginger for 1 minute. Add the chicken and stir-fry rapidly for 2 minutes.

3. Add the onion, green chili, and soy sauce and continue to stir-fry for 1 minute. Add the egg white and stir-fry for 1 minute. Add the scallion and coriander. Mix well and remove from the heat.

Serve warm with other dishes.

SERVES 4

Note: Should you wish a more pungent, hot chili taste, add ½ teaspoon of dried hot red chili flakes when you fry the ginger and garlic. Do not use the green chili.

Also, one whole breast of Cornish hen may be used in this recipe, about 1 cup of cubes.

KYETTHA LON CHO CHIN

Chicken Balls in Sweet Tamarind Sauce

This is a fine party dish, which can be doubled or tripled to accommodate a larger guest list.

SAUCE

> 1 tablespoon tamarind paste, soaked in ¼ cup water for 20
>   minutes, and strained
> 3 teaspoons sugar
> 2 teaspoons rice flour
> 2 teaspoons fish sauce

CHICKEN BALLS

> ½ pound boneless chicken
> 2 garlic cloves, chopped fine
> 2 teaspoons rice flour
> ½ teaspoon salt
> 2 teaspoons fish sauce
> 3 tablespoons corn or peanut oil
> 1 cup shredded cabbage
> ¼ cup chicken broth
> ½ cup thin diagonal slices of celery
> ¼ cup ½-inch cubes of sweet red or green pepper
> 1 scallion, sliced
> ¼ cup coarse-chopped fresh coriander

1. Make the tamarind sauce by adding the sugar, rice flour, and fish sauce to the tamarind liquid. Set aside.

2. Process the chicken, half of the chopped garlic, the rice flour, and salt together into a paste. After dipping your fingers into the fish sauce, shape the chicken mixture into balls 1 inch in diameter.

3. Heat 2 tablespoons of the oil in a skillet and brown the balls over moderate heat for 3 minutes. Set aside.

4. Heat remaining tablespoon of oil in a large skillet or wok and brown the rest of the fine-chopped garlic over moderate heat. Add the cabbage and stir-fry for 2 minutes.

5. Add the chicken balls, stir-fry for 1 minute, and add the tamarind sauce. Stir-fry for 1 minute, then add the chicken broth, celery, sweet pepper, scallion, and coriander. Stir-fry for 2 minutes to combine the ingredients.

Serve warm with other dishes.

SERVES 4

THABUT THI KYETTHA KYAW CHET

Chicken and Zucchini Stir-Fry

1 cup ½-inch cubes of boneless chicken
2 teaspoons soy sauce
½ teaspoon salt
½ teaspoon sugar
1 tablespoon corn or peanut oil
1 garlic clove, chopped
½ to 1 teaspoon sliced fresh hot green chili
1 pound zucchini, cut into ¼-inch-thick slices
½ cup water

1. Marinate the chicken with the soy sauce, salt, and sugar for 15 minutes.

2. Heat the oil in a wok or skillet and lightly brown the garlic. Add the chicken and stir-fry over moderate heat for 3 minutes. Add the chili and zucchini and continue to stir-fry for 2 minutes.

3. Add the water, stir well, cover the pan, and simmer for 5 minutes. Uncover, and stir well for a moment.

Serve warm.

SERVES 4

Note: Other vegetables that may be used in place of zucchini are ridge gourd, bitter melon, and yellow summer squash.

BETHE ACHO CHET

Sweet Cooked Duck

1 duck, 4 to 4½ pounds
2 tablespoons soy sauce
1 teaspoon salt
1 tablespoon corn or peanut oil
6 whole peppercorns
2 tablespoons brown sugar
1 inch of fresh ginger, chopped fine
2 garlic cloves, chopped fine
1 teaspoon bean paste
3 cups water

1. Cut the duck into 8 or 10 serving pieces. Remove loose skin and fat. Pull out and discard rib bones and use the back for another purpose if you wish. Marinate the duck pieces in the soy sauce and salt for 15 minutes.

2. Heat the oil in a large heavy pan with a cover. Add the peppercorns and brown sugar and stir over moderate heat to melt the sugar.

3. Add the ginger and garlic and stir-fry for 1 minute. Add the duck pieces and brown for 10 minutes, covered.

4. Add the bean paste, mix well, and add the water. Bring to a boil and cook over moderate heat for about 45 minutes, until the duck is tender and almost all the liquid has evaporated.

Pour off as much fat as possible and serve the duck warm with rice.

SERVES 4

BETHE HIN

Simple Duck Curry

1 duck, 4½ to 5 pounds, with giblets
1 teaspoon salt
1 tablespoon fish sauce
1 teaspoon ground turmeric
3 tablespoons corn or peanut oil
4 garlic cloves, chopped
1 inch of fresh ginger, chopped
2 medium-size onions, chopped coarse, 1 cup
1 tablespoon paprika
3 cups water

1. Cut the duck into serving pieces—legs, thighs, wings divided, breast quartered, back halved. Marinate duck, including giblets, with the salt, fish sauce, and ½ teaspoon turmeric for 30 minutes.

2. Heat the oil in a pan, add ½ teaspoon turmeric, the garlic, and ginger, and stir-fry over moderate heat for 1 minute. Add the onions and paprika and stir-fry the mixture until light brown, about 3 minutes.

3. Add the duck pieces and brown over moderate heat for 10 minutes.

4. Add the water, bring to a boil, cover the pan, and cook until tender, about 1 hour. Adjust salt if necessary.

Serve warm with rice and vegetable dishes.

SERVES 6

Note: American ducks have a lot of fat. At the end of the cooking time, pour off as much fat as possible before serving.

BE PAUNG

Special Festive Stuffed Duck

In my opinion, this delicious stuffed duck is one of the very best ways of preparing duck in all of Asia. A very large claim but deserved.

1 duck, 4 to 4½ pounds

STUFFING
1 tablespoon salt
½ cup soy sauce
1 inch of fresh ginger, chopped fine
2 garlic cloves, chopped fine
1 tablespoon corn or peanut oil
1 tablespoon brown sugar
8 quail eggs, hard cooked, canned or fresh, shelled
2 whole hard-cooked hen's eggs, shelled
8 prepared fish balls, purchased in Oriental shop
6 medium-size shrimps with heads, whole
½ cup ½-inch-cubes of peeled kohlrabi
¼ cup ½-inch pieces of celery
1 duck liver
4 whole shallots, peeled

GLAZE
1 tablespoon honey
2 tablespoons soy sauce

2-inch piece of fresh ginger, sliced
2 quarts water
1 tablespoon salt

1. Remove the loose fat pockets from the duck and dry the interior with a paper towel.

2. Mix the salt, soy sauce, ginger, and garlic together. Set aside.

3. Heat the oil in a skillet, add the brown sugar, and stir-fry for a moment to melt the sugar. Add the quail eggs, hen's eggs, fish balls, and 2 teaspoons of the soy sauce mixture. Stir-fry for 2 minutes.

Remove the eggs and fish balls and set aside, but leave sauce in the skillet.

4. Fry the shrimps in the same skillet for 1 minute on each side. Remove and set aside, but leave the remaining sauce.

5. In the same skillet, stir-fry the kohlrabi over moderate heat for 1 minute. Add the celery and stir-fry for 1 minute more. Set aside.

6. Cook the liver in boiling water in a covered pan for 3 minutes. Remove, cool, and slice into ½-inch pieces. Set aside.

7. Put 2 tablespoons of the soy sauce/ginger/garlic mixture in the duck cavity and shake it around. Mix together the stuffing ingredients—the quail eggs, hen's eggs, fish balls, shrimps, kohlrabi, celery, duck liver, and shallots—and stuff the duck. Sew up the body cavity of the duck but leave the neck open. Through the neck opening pour in the balance of the soy sauce/ginger/garlic mixture and sew up the neck.

At this stage the duck may be refrigerated to be cooked the following day if you wish.

8. Mix the honey with 1 tablespoon soy sauce. Set aside.

9. Bring the ginger, 2 quarts water, the salt, and 1 tablespoon soy sauce to a boil in a large pan over moderate heat. Add the duck, cover the pan, and cook for 45 minutes. Turn the duck over once during this time. Remove from the pan and discard all the liquid.

10. Preheat oven to 400°F. Rub the duck all over with the honey and soy-sauce mixture. Put the duck *breast side down* in a roasting pan and roast uncovered for 30 minutes. Turn the duck over and roast for 30 minutes more. Remove duck and place it under an oven broiler, breast side up, for 3 to 5 minutes more. This will color and crisp the skin.

Serve warm.

SERVES 6

BE SIPYAN

Braised Duck, Shan Style

This recipe is from the picture-postcard Inle Lake where the houses around the perimeter of the lake are on stilts. Ducks are everywhere, swimming before and beneath the houses, diving and fishing. Both their meat and eggs, especially the eggs, are highly prized.

1 duck, 4 to 4½ pounds, with giblets
2 medium-size onions, sliced thin, 1 cup
3 garlic cloves, sliced thin
½ inch of fresh ginger, sliced thin
1 tablespoon soy sauce
½ teaspoon salt
2 teaspoons lemon juice
¼ teaspoon ground turmeric
1 teaspoon garam masala
1 teaspoon shrimp paste
1 teaspoon chopped fresh hot green chili
1 tablespoon corn or peanut oil
2½ cups water

1. Cut the duck into 8 pieces. Remove loose skin and fat. Dry the pieces on paper towels. Marinate duck and giblets in the other combined ingredients, except the water, in a large pan for 15 minutes.

2. Cook the duck and marinade over moderate heat for 5 minutes, then reduce heat to low. Stir well and add 1 cup water. Cover the pan and cook the duck slowly for 30 minutes.

3. Add 1½ cups water and continue to cook slowly until duck is tender and the water has almost evaporated, leaving a thick, spicy sauce. Total cooking time is about 1 hour and 15 minutes. Pour off as much oil and fat as possible.

Serve warm with rice and other dishes.

SERVES 4 TO 6

BE OO HIN

Dry Egg Curry

This curry is a side dish, usually served with a variety of other characteristic Burmese dishes.

6 eggs
1 teaspoon chopped fresh ginger
1 garlic clove
1 small onion, chopped, ¼ cup
2 teaspoons shrimp powder
½ teaspoon shrimp paste
½ teaspoon paprika
½ teaspoon dried hot red chili flakes
3 tablespoons corn or peanut oil
⅛ teaspoon ground turmeric
2 tablespoons fish sauce
½ teaspoon salt
¼ cup water

1. Cook the eggs in their shells for 5 minutes after the water has
come to a boil. Drain. Soak the eggs in cold water for 10 minutes.
Peel the eggs and cut them lengthwise into halves. The yolks will be
half-cooked.

2. In a processor, crush together the ginger, garlic, onion, shrimp
powder, shrimp paste, paprika, and chili flakes, just to combine.

3. Heat the oil in a skillet, add turmeric, and place egg halves,
yolk side down, in the oil. Fry for 2 minutes, turn the halves over,
and fry for 1 minute more. Remove eggs and set aside.

4. In the same skillet, fry the crushed spice mixture over moderate
heat for 2 minutes. Add the fish sauce and salt and fry for 1 minute
more.

5. Return eggs to the skillet, add the water, and cook for 3 minutes,
shaking the pan vigorously enough to keep the eggs from sticking but
not enough to break the yolks.

Serve warm or at room temperature with other dishes.

SERVES 6

SIDE PAU BE-OO KYAW

Omelet with Pickled Turnip

The lightly preserved, crunchy, pickled turnip is purchased packaged in any Chinatown shop. It adds both texture and flavor to a simple omelet.

3 large eggs, well beaten
2 tablespoons pickled turnip, chopped coarse
1 scallion, sliced thin
½ teaspoon salt
1 tablespoon corn or peanut oil

1. Mix everything together except the oil.

2. Heat half of the oil in a skillet and pour in half of the egg mixture. Over moderate heat, fry the omelet for a minute, fold it over, and fry for 2 minutes more. Prepare 2 omelets this way.

Serve warm with other dishes.

SERVES 4

Variation: The egg batter may also be steamed. Oil each cup in a 6- or 8-cup muffin pan. Fill each cup almost to the top with the egg batter. Steam in a Chinese-style steamer over moderate heat for 15 minutes to produce individual steamed custards.

OO-HNAUK KYAW

Brain Omelet

For brain lovers, and there are many, this omelet can make an excellent lunch, served with a simple Burmese soup and salad.

> 1 beef brain, about 1 pound
> 2 tablespoons corn or peanut oil
> 1 small onion, sliced, ¼ cup
> ½ teaspoon salt
> 2 teaspoons soy sauce
> 2 eggs, beaten
> Ground pepper

1. Soak the brain in cold water and carefully remove the membrane. Cut the brain into ½-inch pieces.

2. Heat the oil in a skillet and over moderate heat fry the onion for 2 minutes. Add the brain, salt, and soy sauce and stir-fry for 3 to 4 minutes.

3. Pour the eggs over all and shake the pan to settle the mixture. Fry for 3 minutes, turn the omelet over, and fry for 1 minute more. Sprinkle with ground pepper.

Serve warm with rice or bread.

SERVES 4

FISH AND SEAFOOD

Fish is the most popular food of the Burmese. This is logical since the Bay of Bengal, which stretches the entire length of the country, provides fish in great quantity and variety and also cheap in price. Shrimps and prawns are the most popular seafood, but lobster is also found in great quantities. The quality is first rate because it moves from the fisherman's net to the wok or skillet so rapidly. Very small shrimps are dried and used particularly as a flavoring. Markets even have dried shrimp sections where they are displayed according to color—pink, salmon, or bright orange. You judge the quality by the color.

It is worth a special trip to that great Scott Market in Rangoon to see the display. The dried shrimp section in that gigantic brick cavern (named after the British Civil Servant, Sir James George Scott, 1851–1935) is a Technicolor showplace, with an aroma to match.

Freshwater fish are also in good supply, especially catfish that thrive in the great Irrawaddy River and in the other streams all over Burma. It is a matter of geographical good luck that the Burmese have this vast amount of fish and seafood, and because Burma is not overpopulated like its neighbor India, nor has it spawned an insatiable fishing industry, the supply may be safe.

The Burmese have matched the abundance of fish with a corresponding quantity of recipes that are imaginative and varied. This gives us one of the most valuable chapters in this book.

NGA MOAT KYAW

Fried Atlantic Pompano

Pompano is a meaty fish of fine flavor. It is found in large schools in the waters of Burma, as is *permit*, a similar fish the Burmese would use in this recipe. Here we would use the pompano found off the coast of Florida and in the Gulf of Mexico.

1 pound pompano, trimmed of fins, cut into 2-inch-wide strips
⅛ teaspoon ground turmeric
½ teaspoon salt
Oil for deep-frying
1 small onion, sliced
1 medium-size ripe tomato, sliced
1 tablespoon soy sauce
2 tablespoons water
2 tablespoons chopped coriander

1. Marinate the fish with the turmeric and salt for 15 minutes.

2. Heat oil in a skillet and deep-fry the fish slices for 3 minutes. Remove them from the oil. Remove all the oil except 1 tablespoon.

3. Over moderate heat, fry the onion and tomato for 1 minute. Add the fish slices, soy sauce, and water and fry for another minute, shaking the pan and turning the fish over. Sprinkle with coriander.

Serve warm or at room temperature with other dishes.

SERVES 4

Variation: The whole fish, including the head, may be prepared in this manner and cooked for 5 minutes additional.

NGA KIN

Smoked Fish

½ teaspoon salt
½ teaspoon fish sauce
¼ teaspoon ground turmeric
2 tablespoons lime or lemon juice
1 to 1½ pounds red snapper, sea bass, boneless grouper, or similar
* fish*

1. Mix the salt, fish sauce, turmeric, and lime juice together. Rub the mixture all over the fish. Let it stand for 10 minutes.

2. Put the fish into an oiled baking dish and bake in a 300°F. oven for 20 minutes.

3. Remove fish from the oven and place it over a charcoal grill for 5 minutes on each side to crisp the skin and produce a smoked flavor. Or the fish may broiled over high heat in an oven broiler for 5 minutes on each side.

Serve warm with other dishes.

SERVES 4

NGA KYAW CHET

Crisp-Fried, Twice-Cooked Fish

The fish has a chewy texture with an unexpected spicy tang. A fine preparation for fish lovers as a main course, as well as being an excellent side dish with a medley of traditional foods at a Burmese meal.

1½ pounds whole sea bass, porgy, or red snapper
½ teaspoon ground turmeric
½ teaspoon salt
3 tablespoons chopped onion
2 garlic cloves, sliced
½ inch of fresh ginger, sliced
1 teaspoon dried hot red chili flakes
1 teaspoon paprika
1 cup oil for deep-frying
1 teaspoon fish sauce

1. Cut diagonal incisions on each side of the fish, 1 inch apart, the length of the fish and to the center bone. Mix the turmeric and salt together and rub it into the incisions and all over the fish. Set aside for 10 minutes.

2. In a processor coarse-chop the onion, garlic, ginger, chili flakes, and paprika together. Set aside.

3. Heat the oil in a skillet and brown-crisp the fish on both sides for 8 to 10 minutes. Remove fish and set aside.

4. Pour off all the oil except 2 tablespoons. Fry the onion mixture over moderate heat until brown, adding the fish sauce.

5. Return fish to the skillet long enough to push the spice mixture into the incisions on both sides and fry for 1 minute.

Serve at room temperature with other dishes.

SERVES 4

NGA WETMA KYAW

Fried Grouper Slices

The firm-textured, meaty grouper makes an admirable appetizer when batter-fried. It holds together when picked up with your fingers and combines the taste and texture of both meat and fish. It is compatible with any type of Burmese dip.

½ pound grouper, cut into strips 2 inches long and ¼ inch thick
1 tablespoon lemon juice
¼ teaspoon salt
⅛ teaspoon pepper
1 egg, beaten
1 tablespoon cold water
2 tablespoons flour
1 teaspoon soy sauce
Oil for deep-frying

1. Marinate the fish with the lemon juice, salt, and pepper for 15 minutes.

2. Prepare a batter by thoroughly mixing together the egg, water, flour, and soy sauce.

3. Heat the oil in a wok or skillet. Dip the fish slices into the batter and brown in the oil over moderate heat for 2 to 3 minutes. Drain on paper towels.

Serve warm as a side dish or as an appetizer with drinks.

SERVES 4

NGA PENGAPI

Crisp-Fried Fish in Seasoned Sauce

2 pounds whole porgy, red snapper, or sea bass
2 teaspoons salt
¼ teaspoon ground turmeric
¼ cup corn or peanut oil, or more
4 garlic cloves, sliced thin lengthwise
1 teaspoon thin julienne slices of fresh ginger
1 medium-size onion, sliced, ½ cup
1 medium-size ripe tomato, sliced, ½ cup
2 teaspoons bean paste
1 tablespoon soy sauce
1 cup water

1. Cut diagonal slashes 1 inch apart on both sides of the fish. The cuts should just touch the center bone. Mix the salt and turmeric together and rub it over the fish and into the cuts. Let stand for 15 minutes.

2. Heat the oil in a large skillet and fry the whole fish over moderate heat until crispy brown on both sides, 10 to 12 minutes. Remove the fish to a platter. Discard all but 2 tablespoons of the oil.

3. Heat the oil and fry the garlic, ginger, and onion for 2 minutes. Add the tomato and stir-fry for 2 minutes more. Add the bean paste and soy sauce and stir-fry for another minute. Add the water and cook the sauce over moderate heat for 5 minutes.

4. Return the fish to the sauce and baste it for 2 minutes.

Serve the fish and sauce warm.

SERVES 4 TO 6

NGA-YEYO-YWET

Swiss Chard and Fish Sticks

This dish is traditionally cooked with catfish (*nagakhu*), which is found in the freshwater rivers. It is a meaty firm fish, and does not break up when cooked. Catfish in Burma are also caught in saltwater and these are much larger than their freshwater cousins.

½ pound fillet of flounder, red snapper, catfish or similar fish
½ teaspoon salt
¼ teaspoon ground turmeric
2 tablespoons corn or peanut oil
2 tablespoons sliced onion
1 garlic clove, chopped
½ teaspoon shrimp paste
2 teaspoons fish sauce
¼ teaspoon paprika
2 teaspoons thin-sliced fresh hot green chili
¼ pound Swiss chard, leaves only, cut into ¼-inch-wide slices,
    about 4 cups

1. Cut the fillet into sticks ¼ inch wide, about 2 inches long. Marinate these with ¼ teaspoon salt and ⅛ teaspoon turmeric. Set aside for 15 minutes.

2. Heat the oil in a large skillet, add remaining ¼ teaspoon salt and ⅛ teaspoon turmeric, the onion, and garlic, and stir-fry over moderate heat for 2 minutes.

3. Add the fish sticks, shrimp paste, fish sauce, paprika, and chili, adjusting the amount of chili to taste. Stir-fry carefully for 2 minutes.

4. Add the Swiss chard and stir-fry carefully, so as not to break up the fish, for 2 minutes longer.

Serve warm with rice.

SERVES 2

SADAW NGA HTOK

King's Steamed Fish Delight

This is another 120-year-old recipe from the kitchen of King Mindon, who reigned in Mandalay. The recipe has been reconstructed from an old book and is authentic.

*1 pound fillet of flounder or similar fish, cut into slices 1 inch long
     and ½ inch wide
1 teaspoon fresh ginger juice
2 teaspoons fine-chopped garlic
½ teaspoon salt
2 eggs, beaten
5 tablespoons diced onion
1 tablespoon corn or peanut oil
2 teaspoons shrimp paste
Pinch of pepper
¼ teaspoon roasted salt
6-inch banana leaves (optional)
8-inch-square aluminum foil sheets*

1. Mix the fish with the ginger juice, 1 teaspoon of the garlic, the salt, eggs, and 2 tablespoons of diced onion. Heat the oil in a skillet and stir-fry the mixture over moderate heat for 2 minutes. Remove from heat.

2. Add the rest of the garlic and onion, the shrimp paste, pepper, and roasted salt to the fish mixture. Stir well.

3. Place a banana leaf, if used, on a square of foil. Add ½ cup of the fish mixture. Fold the foil and leaf over to prepare a 4-inch-square package. Continue with the rest of the fish mixture. Steam the packages in a Chinese-style steamer for 20 minutes.

Unfold the packages and serve the fish warm.

MAKES 7 OR 8 PACKAGES

NGAYAN PHETHTOAT

Steamed Fish Envelope in Coconut Cream

1 pound fillet of scrod, flounder, sole, or similar fish
⅔ cup Coconut Cream (see Index)
1 teaspoon rice flour
½ cup chopped onion
½ cup thin-sliced onion
¼ teaspoon ground turmeric
¼ teaspoon paprika
½ teaspoon salt
½ inch of fresh ginger, chopped
1 garlic clove, chopped
1 tablespoon thin-sliced fresh semihot green chili
2 teaspoons fish sauce
6 to 8 large cabbage leaves, 2 inches of the hard center core
    removed
6 pieces of aluminum foil, each 12 inches square

1. Cut the fish into 6 pieces, about 3-inch rectangles.

2. Thoroughly mix the coconut cream, rice flour, both chopped and sliced onion, turmeric, paprika, salt, ginger, garlic, chili, and fish sauce together. Add the fish pieces, mix well, and marinate for 15 minutes.

3. In the palm of your hand prepare a pocket with a cabbage leaf. Put a fish rectangle in the center and add 3 tablespoons of the coconut cream mixture. Wrap up the leaf, place it firmly in a sheet of aluminum foil, fold over both ends toward the middle, and tightly fold over the sides to create a sealed envelope. Prepare 6 envelopes this way.

4. Steam the envelopes in a Chinese-style steamer over moderate heat for 25 minutes.

Serve warm. Serve the foil package on a platter, unfold, and eat the contents while still in the envelope.

SERVES 4

Note: Traditionally the envelopes are wrapped in banana leaves, which are not eaten.

Variations: Large Swiss chard leaves are a good substitute for the banana leaves. They are flexible for wrapping and are edible.

Shelled and deveined shrimps make a good substitute for the fish rectangles. Use 1 pound medium shrimps and divide them equally into the 6 envelopes with the coconut cream mixture. Steam for 25 minutes as for the fish.

NGA PENGAPE

Quick-Cook Fish Fillet

This is a simple, quick stir-fry with Oriental flavors. All the ingredients are fresh-tasting without heavy-duty spices to interfere with the subtlety of the fish fillet.

2 tablespoons corn or peanut oil
1 large green, red, or yellow sweet pepper, cut into 2-inch julienne
    strips, about 1 cup
3 scallions, cut into 1-inch pieces
1 pound fillet of flounder, sole, scrod, or red snapper, cut into 2-
    inch pieces
1 teaspoon bean paste
1 tablespoon soy sauce
½ cup water
2 tablespoons chopped fresh coriander

1. Heat the oil in a large skillet and stir-fry the sweet pepper and scallions over moderate heat for 1 minute.

2. Add the fish pieces, one by one, and fry without stirring for 1 minute. Dissolve the bean paste in the soy sauce and sprinkle it over the fish. Shake the pan vigorously for a moment.

3. Pour the water over the fish, shake the pan several times, and continue to fry for 3 minutes. Sprinkle the coriander over all.

Serve warm with rice.

SERVES 4

NGATHALAUK PAUNG

Melted-Bone Shad

This is an extraordinary preparation for several reasons. Shad, which is famous for its roe, is also infamous for its many small bones and because of that, it is difficult to prepare in Western style. (American shad is the largest member of the herring family—*Alosa sapidissima.*)

In India-Burma, a close relative, known as *hilsa*, is much sought after during the season. In my years of residence in Calcutta, my cook would laboriously remove the small bones in *hilsa* fillet with tweezers, then grill or smoke it. Incomparable!

The Burmese have solved the bone situation. Cooking shad their way literally melts the bones without altering the texture of the fish, which remains smooth, rich and melting, dark and meaty. One can eat the center bone, and even the head becomes soft and deliciously edible.

A Burmese proverb says: "When you select a fish to eat, choose *hilsa* (shad); when you select a wife, choose a teenager."

1 shad, about 3 pounds

MARINADE
> *¼ cup lemon juice*
> *2 tablespoons fish sauce*
> *⅛ teaspoon ground turmeric*
> *½ teaspoon salt*
> *½ teaspoon paprika*

SAUCE
> *2 tablespoons corn or peanut oil*
> *1 small onion, chopped fine, ¼ cup*
> *2 garlic cloves, chopped fine*
> *1 inch of fresh ginger, chopped fine*
> *1 medium-size ripe tomato, chopped, about ½ cup*
> *1½ cups water*

1. Cut the shad into 3-inch-wide slices, including the head. Score the pieces vertically on each side of each slice. Cut deep to the center bone to allow the marinade to enter.

2. Mix the lemon juice, fish sauce, turmeric, salt, and paprika together. Pour it over the shad and rub it into the pieces. Marinate everything overnight, refrigerated.

3. Heat the oil in a skillet and over moderate heat stir-fry the onion, garlic, ginger, and tomato for 3 minutes. Add the fish and marinade, mix well, and stir-fry for 5 minutes. Add the water.

4. Turn the fish and sauce into a heatproof dish and place it in a pressure cooker. (Or put the fish directly into the pressure cooker.) Cook over moderately low heat for 1½ hours.

Another method is to cook the fish and sauce in a pan with a tight cover over moderately low heat for 3 hours. Add more water if necessary.

Serve warm with rice.

SERVES 6

NGA HIN

Simple Fish Curry

This is a simple curry to make, especially since the fillet does not take many minutes to cook. Browning the onion, garlic, and ginger together so that they become nearly crisp provides the intensity of flavor in the sauce. This is a relatively dry curry since most of the liquid will evaporate.

1 pound fillet of flounder, sole, or scrod, cut into 2-inch pieces
⅛ teaspoon ground turmeric
½ teaspoon salt
2 teaspoons fish sauce
3 tablespoons corn or peanut oil
1 small onion, sliced, ¼ cup
1 garlic clove, chopped fine
½ inch of fresh ginger, chopped fine
½ teaspoon paprika
1 ripe tomato, chopped, ½ cup
¼ cup water
2 tablespoons chopped fresh coriander

1. Marinate the fish with turmeric, salt, and 1 teaspoon fish sauce. Rub the seasonings into each piece of fish. Let stand for 15 minutes.

2. Heat the oil in a large skillet and stir-fry the onion, garlic, and ginger over moderate heat until light brown, about 3 minutes. Add the paprika, stir for a moment, then add the tomato and remaining 1 teaspoon fish sauce. Stir-fry the mixture for 2 minutes to cook the tomato.

3. Add the fish pieces, one by one, and fry for 2 minutes without turning them. Add the water and shake the pan vigorously to mix the flavors. Do not stir or the fish will break up.

4. Cook for 2 minutes more and sprinkle with coriander.

Serve warm with white rice.

SERVES 4

NGA WETMA
Fish Curry

The grouper is an extremely large fish with a thick skin. The flesh is wonderfully meaty, slightly dark, with a texture that is chewy rather than tender. The Burmese name for this fish, which is found in abundance in Burmese waters, is "female pig," supposedly reflecting its meaty texture and large size, also the rather long face and head.

The spotted grouper is the largest and may reach a weight of 700 pounds. I have seen huge slabs of the fish laid out in New York's Chinatown while slices were being eagerly purchased by Asian buyers.

1 pound boneless grouper, cut into 1-inch cubes
1 teaspoon paprika
¼ teaspoon ground turmeric
½ teaspoon salt
3 teaspoons fish sauce
2 tablespoons corn or peanut oil
2 tablespoons fine-chopped onion
½ inch of fresh ginger, chopped fine
2 garlic cloves, chopped fine
1 cup cubed tomatoes, fresh or canned
⅔ cup water
2 tablespoons chopped fresh coriander
2 small fresh hot green chilies, sliced thin

1. Marinate the fish with ½ teaspoon paprika, ⅛ teaspoon turmeric, the salt, and 1 teaspoon fish sauce for 15 minutes.

2. Heat the oil in a pan and fry the onion, ginger, garlic, and the rest of the turmeric and paprika over moderate heat for 2 minutes. Add the tomatoes and remaining fish sauce, and stir-fry for 3 minutes to reduce the mixture to a purée.

3. Add the fish and stir-fry it and the sauce until the color changes. Add the water, stir a moment, cover the pan, and cook over low heat for 20 minutes to evaporate the liquid and create a thick sauce.

4. Sprinkle the curry with the coriander and chilies.

Serve warm with rice and other dishes.

SERVES 4

NGA PHE KYAW

Basic Fish Cake

The traditional way of preparing the fish for this recipe is to pound it in a stone mortar with a pestle. The fish is crushed, rather than cut small as it is in a processor. In preparing this recipe, I processed the fish and seasonings until smooth, then continued with mortar and pestle and pounded the mixture for 5 minutes more. The texture, which should be slightly rubbery, was very close to that of the Burmese.

4 garlic cloves, sliced
½ inch of fresh ginger, sliced
1½ pounds boneless kingfish, flounder, or similar fish
½ teaspoon ground turmeric
½ teaspoon paprika
½ teaspoon salt
1 tablespoon fish sauce
¼ cup corn or peanut oil

1. Pound the garlic and ginger together in a mortar or process to a smooth paste in a food processor. Add the fish, which has been cut into 2-inch slices, and continue to process or pound to a smooth fish paste or dough.

2. Add turmeric, paprika, and salt, and continue to process these into the fish. The success of this recipe depends upon a thorough pounding, which might take about 15 minutes.

3. To prepare fish cakes, moisten your fingers with the fish sauce and shape cakes 3 inches in diameter and ½ inch thick. Smooth the cakes over by dabbing lightly with fish sauce.

4. Heat the oil in a skillet and brown the fish cakes over moderate heat for about 3 minutes on each side. Drain them on paper towels.

Serve them warm or set aside to use in other preparations.

MAKES 6 CAKES

Note: To boil fish cakes, prepare cakes according to the basic recipe. Bring ½ cup water to a boil and cook the fish cakes covered, for 2 minutes on each side. Drain well and cool before slicing.

NGAPHE THOAT

Fish Cake Salad

1 *medium-size onion, sliced thin,* ½ *cup*
1 *boiled Basic Fish Cake (see Index), cut into* ¼-*inch-thick slices*
½ *fresh semihot green chili, sliced thin*
1 *tablespoon coarse-chopped fresh coriander*
1 *scallion, sliced thin*
1 *tablespoon Crispy Fried Onions (see Index), plus 1 tablespoon oil
     from the recipe*
½ *cup julienne pieces of young cucumber, not peeled*
2 *tablespoons lime or lemon juice, preferably lime*
1 *teaspoon fish sauce*
¼ *teaspoon salt*

1. Rinse the onion in cold water and press dry on paper towels.

2. Place the fish cake slices, onion, green chili, coriander, scallion, crispy onion, and cucumber in separate piles on a flat plate to make a decorative arrangement. At table, mix them all together with the lime juice, fish sauce, salt, and flavored oil from the crispy onions. Toss the salad to mix.

Serve at room temperature.

SERVES 4

NGA-PHE WETTHAYAUNG

Fish Cakes in Coconut Cream

"Imitation pork" is the nickname for this dish since the fish cakes look like, and take on the texture of, cooked pork. This dish is prepared for Muslims or for anyone who does not eat pork.

1 medium-size onion, sliced, ½ cup
2 garlic cloves, sliced
¼ inch of fresh ginger, sliced
½ teaspoon paprika
¼ teaspoon ground turmeric
½ teaspoon salt
½ teaspoon dried hot red chili flakes
1 tablespoon corn or peanut oil
3 fried fish cakes (Basic Fish Cake, see Index), cut into ¼-inch-
    thick slices
1 teaspoon fish sauce
2 tablespoons thick Coconut Cream (see Index)

1. In a processor crush the onion, garlic, ginger, paprika, turmeric, salt, and chili together into a paste.

2. Heat the oil in a skillet and over moderate heat fry the paste for 2 minutes. Add the fish cake pieces and stir them into the mixture for 2 minutes.

3. Add the fish sauce and coconut cream and stir-fry for 2 minutes more.

Serve warm as a side dish.

SERVES 4

INLE NGA HTAMIN NE

Inle Lake Mashed Rice and Fish

Inle Lake is the famous, pictorial lake in Upper Burma in the region of Taunggyi, the capital of the Shan State. This is a hearty and very tasty snack for any time one is hungry.

1 cup water
2 tablespoons fish sauce
½ teaspoon salt
¼ teaspoon ground turmeric
½ pound fillet of flounder, sole, or similar fish
2 cups warm cooked rice
Crispy Garlic Slices (see Index)
Garlic oil
Whole scallions
Crispy pork skin
Coriander stalks

1. Bring water, fish sauce, salt, and turmeric to a boil. Add the fish, cover the pan, and cook over moderate heat for 10 minutes. Remove the fish.

2. Mash the rice and fish together with a potato ricer. Take ½ cup of the mixture and press it gently into a plate to make a serving ¾ inch thick.

3. Garnish to taste, with crispy garlic slices and oil, scallions, pork skin, and fresh coriander. Indian leek can also be included.

SERVES 6

BE-OO CHIN YE

Egg, Dried Fish, and Potato Stew

This is an interesting and flavorful "meaty" dish, made without meat. The potatoes absorb the flavor of the dried fish and the flavorings, and the eggs add another texture. Traditionally duck eggs are used. They are not completely hard-cooked so that when halved the yolks will still be soft. Frying the eggs firms the texture and makes it possible later on to stir the dish without breaking them up.

> ¼ pound dried cod or similar fish, cut into 2-inch pieces
> 8 eggs
> ¼ cup corn or peanut oil
> 2 tablespoons chopped onion
> 2 garlic cloves, chopped
> ½ inch of fresh ginger, chopped
> ¼ teaspoon ground turmeric
> 1 teaspoon paprika
> ½ to 1 teaspoon dried hot red chili flakes
> 1 tablespoon shrimp paste
> 1 pound potatoes, about 3, peeled, cut into 1-inch cubes
> 2 teaspoons fish sauce
> 3 cups water
> 2 tablespoons tamarind paste, dissolved in ½ cup water and
>   strained

1. Cover the dried fish with water, soak for 1 hour, and drain.

2. Cook the eggs in their shells for 8 minutes. Drain them under cold water, peel, and cut them into halves.

3. Heat the oil in a skillet and over moderate heat fry the eggs, yolk side down, for 2 minutes. Turn eggs over and brown the other sides. Remove eggs and set aside.

4. In the same oil over moderate heat, fry the onion, garlic, ginger, turmeric, and paprika for 2 minutes. Add the chili flakes and shrimp paste and stir-fry for 2 minutes more.

5. Add the drained fish, the potatoes, fish sauce, water, and tamarind liquid. Cover the pan and cook for 10 minutes.

6. Add the eggs and cook for 20 minutes more.

Serve warm with rice and other dishes.

SERVES 6

NGA-NITU KYAW
Crisp-Fried Dried Fish

This fish is traditionally served at Water Festival time with Water Festival Rice and Mango Salad (see Index for recipes).

½ pound dried fish, domestic or imported from Asia
1 cup water
Oil for deep-frying, 1 cup
⅛ teaspoon ground turmeric
½ cup Crispy Fried Onions (see Index)
2 tablespoons whole dried hot red chili, toasted

1. Cover the fish with water in a pan. Bring to a boil and cook for 10 minutes to tenderize the fish. Drain well. Shred the fish, removing any bones.

2. Heat the oil, add the turmeric, and stir for a few minutes. Add the fish shreds and fry over moderate heat until crispy and brown. Remove and drain on paper towels.

3. Mix the fish and onions together.

Serve on a plate at room temperature, garnished with hot chili.

SERVES 4

NGA STEW

Fish Stew

This is an Anglo-Burmese recipe, with flavorings and ingredients being entirely English. It was originally served in Colonial Burma to the English, who were nostalgic for familiar foods of home. It is delicious.

1 tablespoon butter
1 pound fillet of red snapper, flounder, sole, or similar fish, cut into
*   1-inch cubes*
1 cup milk
2 bay leaves
1 medium-size carrot, sliced
¼ pound cauliflower, cut into 1-inch pieces, 2 cups
½ teaspoon salt

1. Heat the butter in a skillet or pan and lightly fry the cubes of fish for 2 minutes. Add the milk, bay leaves, carrot, cauliflower, and salt.

2. Simmer, covered, over moderately low heat for 15 minutes.

Serve warm as a first course with bread.

SERVES 4

Variation: Shrimps provide an excellent substitute for the fish. Peel and devein 1 pound medium shrimps and proceed in the same manner as for the fish cubes.

NGA GUANG HIN

Fish-Head Curry

One should concentrate on the flavor and not the beauty of this curry. One of my favorite curries, it should be cooked at home where one can pick over the fish head, extracting all of the fish and goodness locked in the bones, without losing social status.

2 fish heads, 2 pounds, quartered—tilefish, red snapper, or similar meaty fish
½ cup chopped onion
2 garlic cloves, chopped
½ inch of fresh ginger, chopped
1 medium-size tomato, quartered, about ½ cup
2 tablespoons fish sauce
½ teaspoon ground turmeric
2 teaspoons paprika
1 teaspoon salt
¼ cup corn or peanut oil
1 heaping tablespoon tamarind paste, dissolved in ½ cup water and strained
½ cup fresh coriander, chopped
½ fresh semihot green chili, sliced

1. Marinate the fish head with onion, garlic, ginger, tomato, fish sauce, turmeric, paprika, salt, and oil for 15 minutes. Mix well.

2. Lightly cook the mixture in a covered pan over moderate heat for 15 minutes.

3. Add the tamarind liquid and cook for 10 minutes more. Shake the pan back and forth. Do not stir or the fish will disintegrate.

4. Lastly, add the coriander and chili and cook for 5 minutes more.

Serve warm with rice.

SERVES 4

PAZUN KYA

Tiger Prawns

This is an easily prepared traditional dish. Tiger prawns are large shrimps, darkly striped like a tiger, therefore the name. Any large whole shrimps may be used.

Most shrimps are sold in the United States without heads, and therefore the head oil, which intensifies the flavor and color of the shrimp, is lost. This dish really requires the head oil to give it the full seasoning and therefore it is well worth tracking down a source of whole shrimps. Shrimp-head oil is considered a luxurious delicacy in Burma.

>*1 pound whole fresh tiger prawns with heads*
>*½ teaspoon salt*
>*⅛ teaspoon ground turmeric*
>*1 tablespoon corn or peanut oil*
>*2 garlic cloves, sliced thin horizontally*
>*1 tablespoon water*

1. Shell and devein the shrimps. Pull off the heads and scoop out the orange-colored oil. Add the oil to the shrimps. Add the salt and turmeric and mix all together.

2. Heat the oil in a skillet, add the garlic, and fry until it turns yellow. Add the shrimps and stir-fry for 2 minutes. Add the water and continue to stir-fry for about 2 minutes more. The water will evaporate and the shrimp become orange-colored.

Serve warm with other dishes.

SERVES 4

PAZUN SIPYAN

Red Shrimps

In New York's Chinatown and in some other areas of the country, it is possible to buy fresh whole shrimps with heads. These shrimps have a more authentic flavor, and should be used when available for all Burmese cooking.

In Burma, both freshwater and saltwater shrimps and prawns are available, but the freshwater shrimps are the most delicious.

1 pound large shrimps with heads on, peeled and deveined
1 tablespoon corn or peanut oil
⅛ teaspoon ground turmeric
½ cup thin-sliced onion
1 garlic clove, chopped fine or crushed
¼ inch of fresh ginger, crushed
1 teaspoon paprika
2 teaspoons fish sauce
2 tablespoons chopped tomato
½ teaspoon salt

1. Take off the shrimp head, which contains excellent flavor, and clip off the pointed nose. Also, remove the small black sac found in the head and discard it.

2. Heat the oil in a wok or skillet, add the turmeric, onion, garlic, ginger, and paprika, and stir-fry over moderate heat for 3 minutes to brown the onion lightly.

3. Add the fish sauce, tomato, and salt, and stir-fry for 1 minute. Add the shrimps and the shrimp heads and stir-fry for 4 minutes to combine the flavors.

Serve warm with rice and other dishes.

SERVES 4 TO 6

KACUN-YET KYAW

Shrimp and Water Spinach Stir-Fry

Burmese love garlic, sometimes chopped coarse enough so that they may bite into the pieces. The garlic in this recipe is added toward the end of the cooking time to intensify its flavor. It certainly does.

2 teaspoons corn or peanut oil
2 tablespoons sliced onion
½ pound small shrimps, peeled and deveined
2 teaspoons fish sauce
½ teaspoon salt
1 pound water spinach, stems, leaves cut into 2-inch lengths
1 garlic clove, chopped fine

1. Heat the oil in a wok or skillet and stir-fry the onion over moderate heat for 1 minute. Add the shrimps, fish sauce, and salt and stir-fry for 2 minutes.

2. Add the water spinach and stir-fry for 2 minutes. Add the garlic and stir-fry for 1 minute more.

Serve warm with other dishes.

SERVES 4

Note: If water spinach is not available, watercress may be used as a substitute.

HMYIT KYAW

Bamboo Shoots, Shrimps, and Garden Pea Sprouts

2 teaspoons corn or peanut oil
¼ teaspoon ground turmeric
1 garlic clove, chopped fine
½ cup ½-inch pieces of peeled and deveined fresh shrimps
1 cup canned bamboo shoots, sliced julienne
2 teaspoons fish sauce
¼ teaspoon salt
½ cup Cooked Garden Pea Sprouts (Pepyoat, see Index)

1. Heat the oil in a skillet and fry the turmeric and garlic over moderate heat for 2 minutes.

2. Add the shrimps and stir-fry for 1 minute. Add the bamboo shoots and stir-fry for another minute.

3. Add the fish sauce, salt, and garden pea sprouts, and stir-fry over moderately low heat for 3 minutes.

Serve warm with other dishes.

SERVES 4

PAZUN KYAW

Shrimp Fry

½ pound medium shrimps, shelled and deveined
¼ teaspoon ground turmeric
½ teaspoon salt
2 tablespoons sliced onion
2 garlic cloves, sliced
½ inch of fresh ginger, sliced
1 teaspoon dried hot red chili flakes
1 teaspoon paprika
2 tablespoons corn or peanut oil
1 teaspoon fish sauce

1. Marinate the shrimps with the turmeric and salt for 5 minutes.

2. Coarse-chop together in a processor the onion, garlic, ginger, chili, and paprika.

3. Heat the oil in a skillet and fry the onion mixture over moderate heat until it is brown and crisp. Add the fish sauce, stir a moment, and add the shrimps. Stir-fry for 5 minutes to cook the shrimps and combine the flavors.

Serve warm with other dishes.

SERVES 4

Note: This dish may also be prepared with small headless shrimps about 1 inch long or smaller. These small shrimps are stir-fried in their shells over high heat and eaten whole, shell and all.

PAZUN SINKAW

Chopped Shrimps in Lime Sauce

The Burmese also eat this shrimp dish raw—just "cooked" by the lime juice. This is the same method encountered in Central and South America where fish and shrimps are soaked in lime or lemon juice and served as *seviche*.

Should you decide to prepare the shrimp as a Burmese *seviche*, eliminate the oil completely, but use 3 tablespoons lime juice (instead of 1 tablespoon) and the other ingredients. Marinate for at least 30 minutes; 1 hour is better. Serve garnished with toasted dried hot red chili flakes and crispy fried onions.

½ pound fresh shrimps, peeled and deveined
1 tablespoon lime juice
½ teaspoon salt
1 small fresh hot green chili, sliced thin
¼ cup ¼-inch dice of sweet red pepper
1 tablespoon corn or peanut oil
2 scallions, green part only, sliced
1 tablespoon chopped fresh coriander

1. Chop the shrimps into coarse pieces. Mix with the lime juice, salt, hot chili, and sweet red pepper. Marinate for 15 minutes.

2. Heat the oil in a skillet, add the shrimps and marinade, and stir-fry for 2 minutes. Add the scallions and coriander and stir-fry over moderate heat for 2 minutes more.

Serve warm as a light snack with other dishes.

SERVES 4

YON PADE THI PAZUN KYAW

Okra and Shrimp Fry

½ pound young okra
¼ pound medium shrimps, shelled and deveined
⅛ teaspoon ground turmeric
¼ teaspoon salt
2 tablespoons corn or peanut oil
2 tablespoons sliced onion
1 garlic clove, sliced
½ semihot red or green chili, sliced
2 scallions, cut into ¼-inch-wide slices
2 teaspoons fish sauce

1. Trim the stems and the tip ends of the okra pods.

2. Mix the shrimps, turmeric, and salt together. Let stand for 15 minutes.

3. Heat the oil in a wok or large skillet and fry the onion and garlic over moderate heat until golden brown. Add the shrimps and stir-fry for 3 minutes.

4. Add the okra, chili, and scallions and continue to stir-fry for 2 minutes. Add the fish sauce and mix well for 1 minute. Do not overcook.

Serve warm with other dishes.

SERVES 4

KA-NYUT PAZUN KYAW

Asparagus and Shrimp Panfry

Surprisingly, Burma produces a great deal of asparagus for local consumption in the tropical highlands. The Burmese love it. During the principal growing season—June, July, and August—large bundles are tied and carted off to the market in Rangoon. When asparagus plants go to seed and produce the tall feathery plants, the Burmese, quoting a poetical saying known as *Shint-Ma-Tet,* call it "The tree that the squirrel can't climb."

1 pound fresh asparagus
½ pound shrimps, peeled and deveined
2 teaspoons fish sauce
¼ teaspoon ground turmeric
½ teaspoon salt
2 teaspoons corn or peanut oil
2 shallots, sliced thin
2 teaspoons soy sauce
½ cup water

1. Trim the asparagus spears and cut them into 2-inch pieces. Peel the tough stem end so that all the hard husk is removed, leaving a tender inner core.

2. Marinate the shrimps with the fish sauce, ⅛ teaspoon turmeric, and the salt. Set aside for 15 minutes.

3. Heat the oil in a skillet. Add remaining ⅛ teaspoon turmeric and the shallots and stir-fry over moderate heat for 2 minutes. Add the asparagus and soy sauce and stir. Add the water, cover the skillet, and cook for about 5 minutes, until the asparagus is tender and the water nearly all evaporated.

4. Add the shrimps and fry for 3 minutes more, mixing them with the asparagus to combine the flavors.

Serve warm.

SERVES 4

PAZUN KONBONGYI

Shrimp, Tofu, and Fish Cake Fry

A Sino-Burmese dish with a memorable combination of flavors.

¼ cup corn or peanut oil
1 Chinese tofu cake, cut into 9 cubes
2 small whole dried hot red chilies
½ pound shrimps, peeled and deveined, cut into ½-inch cubes
2 fish cakes (Basic Fish Cake, see Index), boiled or fried, cut into
    ½-inch cubes
2 teaspoons soy sauce
½ teaspoon salt
1 scallion, cut into 1-inch pieces
2 tablespoons coarse-chopped fresh coriander

1. Heat the oil in a skillet and fry the tofu cubes over moderate heat for 5 minutes, until brown. Remove. Set aside and cut into ½-inch dice.

2. Remove all but 1 tablespoon oil. Fry the chilies in the same skillet over moderate heat for 3 or 4 seconds. Add the shrimps, fish cake cubes, and tofu cubes, and stir-fry for 2 minutes. Add soy sauce and salt and stir-fry for 2 minutes.

3. Lastly, add the scallion and coriander. Stir a moment.

Serve warm with rice and other dishes.

SERVES 4

PEPEPAUK PEPYA PAZUN

Bean-Sprout, Tofu, and Shrimp Stir-Fry

2 Chinese tofu cakes
3 tablespoons corn or peanut oil
2 tablespoons thin-sliced onion
½ pound medium shrimps, shelled and deveined
½ pound bean sprouts
½ teaspoon salt
1 tablespoon soy sauce
1 scallion, cut into ¼-inch slices

1. Cut each tofu cake into 9 cubes. Heat the oil in a skillet and brown the cubes over moderate heat for about 3 minutes. Remove cubes and set aside. Remove all except 1 tablespoon oil.

2. Heat the tablespoon of oil in the skillet and fry the onion over moderate heat for 1 minute. Add the shrimps and stir-fry for 1 minute. Add the bean sprouts, salt, and soy sauce and stir-fry for 3 minutes.

3. Lastly add the tofu cubes and scallion; mix well.

Serve warm with other dishes.

SERVES 4

PYI-GYI NGA KYAW

Fried Squid Rings

½ cup rice flour
1 tablespoon wheat flour
2 teaspoons glutinous rice flour
⅛ teaspoon ground turmeric
½ teaspoon salt
½ cup cold water
Oil for deep-frying
1 pound fresh squids, dressed and cut into ½-inch-wide rings

1. Prepare a batter with the rice flour, wheat flour, glutinous rice flour, turmeric, salt, and water. Mix well and let stand for 15 minutes.

2. Heat the oil in a wok and dip the squid slices into the batter. Fry the slices, one by one, over moderate heat, turning them over to brown lightly on both sides. Do not overfry. Drain on paper towels.

Serve warm with any kind of Burmese dip.

SERVES 4

PYI-GYI NGA KAZUN YWET

Squid and Dandelion Stir-Fry

Watercress and Swiss chard are good substitutes for dandelion since they all have a slightly bitter but appealing taste.

1 teaspoon dried hot red chili flakes
1 tablespoon fresh lemon juice
2 teaspoons soy sauce
1 teaspoon brown sugar
2 teaspoons corn or peanut oil
1 garlic clove, chopped fine
1 pound fresh squids, dressed, cut into ½-inch-round slices
¼ pound dandelion greens, green leaves only, halved

1. Mix the chili flakes, lemon juice, soy sauce, and sugar together. Let stand for 15 minutes.

2. Heat the oil in a wok or skillet and over moderate heat fry the garlic for 1 minute. Add the squid slices and stir-fry for 2 minutes. Add the chili/lemon mixture and continue to fry.

3. Add the dandelion greens and cook for 2 minutes more. Do not overcook since it toughens the squid.

Serve warm with other dishes.

SERVES 4

KIN MON YONPADE THI KYAW

Tofu, Okra, and Squid Stir-Fry

With a few simple ingredients of contrasting flavors and textures, a delectable combination is produced in this easy stir-fry. It is a typical dish of the Chinese community in Lower Burma.

¼ cup corn or peanut oil
1 Chinese tofu cake, cut into 9 cubes
2 garlic cloves, chopped
½ pound squids, dressed and cut into 1-inch pieces
2 cups young okra, cut into 1-inch pieces
2 tablespoons soy sauce

1. Heat the oil in a wok or skillet and brown the tofu cubes over moderate heat. Remove cubes and set aside. Remove all but 1 tablespoon oil.

2. Add the garlic and stir-fry for 1 minute. Add the squid pieces and continue to fry. Add the okra, tofu cubes, and soy sauce and stir-fry the mixture for 2 minutes.

Serve warm with rice.

SERVES 4

PYI-GYI NAG ASA THUT

Stuffed Squid

1 pound squids, 4 to 5 to the pound
1 teaspoon oil
⅛ teaspoon ground turmeric
½ cup ½-inch dice of sweet green pepper
1 shallot, diced
½ cup ½-inch pieces of asparagus
2 teaspoons fish sauce
½ teaspoon salt
2 tablespoons water
2 teaspoons soy sauce
Toothpicks

1. Dress each squid by pulling out the head, tentacles, and the insides. Pull off the outer thin skin membrane. Cut off the tentacles (to use in the stuffing) and cut them into ½-inch pieces with scissors. Rinse out the white, tubular body.

2. Heat the oil in a skillet. Add the turmeric, green pepper, shallot, asparagus, fish sauce, and salt, and stir-fry over moderate heat for 2 minutes. Add the tentacles and stir-fry for 1 minute more.

3. Stuff each squid with some of this mixture. Close the end with a toothpick. Put the squids in a skillet; add the water and the soy sauce. Cover and cook over moderate heat for 3 minutes, or until the liquid evaporates. Turn the squids over once during this time. Cut each squid into 3 pieces.

Serve warm with any suitable Burmese sauce.

SERVES 4

Note: Should asparagus not be available, substitutes may be zucchini, chayote, or okra, cut to the same size as the shallot or green pepper.

PYI-GYI NGA

Squid Salad

In Burma squids are known as "water chicken" and they abound in the coastal waters of the country. This is an ideal recipe for those who prefer a low-fat and high-protein diet.

1 pound squids
1 teaspoon salt
1 teaspoon cornstarch
3 tablespoons cold water
1 teaspoon soy sauce
1 tablespoon tomato ketchup
2 cups fresh spinach, broken up, blanched in hot water for 3
    minutes, drained well

1. Dress the squids, removing the insides and the thin skin, rinsing the tentacles, and discarding the eye. Cut the squid body down the center and open it up in a sort of rectangle. Cut the body into 1-inch-wide strips. Cut the tentacles into 2-inch pieces. (Or buy squid pieces already prepared.)

2. Cook the squid in boiling water with 1 teaspoon salt for 2 minutes. Drain well. Set aside.

3. Dissolve the cornstarch in the cold water with soy sauce and ketchup. Heat briefly in a pan to cook the cornstarch, stirring constantly.

4. Put the squid on one half of a serving platter. Arrange the blanched spinach on the other half. Pour the cornstarch sauce over all.

Serve at room temperature.

SERVES 4

Note: Bottled hot chili sauce, found in Chinese markets, may be added to the cornstarch sauce to make it more peppery. On the other hand, you may prefer to prepare your own Garlic Sauce or Hot Sauce using the recipes with Mandalay Mishee (see Index).

RICE AND PANCAKES

In the world's grain markets, rice is second only to wheat in importance. Prior to World War II, Burma was the world's largest exporter of rice; it is a top producer still. Blessed with an ideal climate, ample rainfall, extensive land area, the farmers have always grown vast quantities for the local population and for export.

Plain, boiled white rice is the staple of Burmese family life. It is eaten in generous quantities at every meal. Fried, seasoned rice dishes of Indian or Chinese origin are common, and rice is cooked in coconut milk for special occasions.

There are many varieties of rice grown in Burma, including a short-grain pink rice and a black, glutinous rice that looks and tastes like our wild rice. I have purchased both of these in the marketplace in Taunggyi, Upper Burma. But they use regular long-grain rice in most dishes, and the glutinous rice (also called sweet or sticky) in preparing sweets and snacks.

Rice flour is prepared from both regular and glutinous rice. The flour is used in making pancake batter and the batter used to coat deep-fried vegetables. Life without rice would be inconceivable to the Burmese.

Every country has its own version of the pancake: Burma's is the 100-Layer Pancake (Htad-Taya, see Index). Plain, Sweet, or Stuffed—all are incomparable as an unusual snack.

THINGYAN HTAMIN

Water Festival Rice

Hnit San is the Burmese New Year and the signal for cleansing the body and mind for the year to come. Large animals are seldom eaten during this period and, in fact, there is general fasting from midday on. Young people noisily celebrate the Water Festival by flinging water at each other from pails, or squirting it from their bicycle pumps. Smoked rice is served with Mango Salad and Crisp-Fried Dried Fish (see Index) in separate dishes. I prefer to add the salad and fish to my rice bowl and eat all together. This preparation is mostly of historical interest, but I hope you will try it.

Sterno
2 cups cooked rice
3 cups water

1. To give the pan and therefore the water a smoky flavor, burn the Sterno inside a pan for 1 minute to produce smoke. Then cover the pan, which extinguishes the flame and produces more smoke. This "seasons" the pan with smoke. Remove the Sterno.

2. Add the rice and water to the pan, cover, and let it stand for 15 minutes. Some of the water will soak into the rice, but it will be soupy. Serve at room temperature.

SERVES 4

PE-HTAMIN

Red Lentils and Rice

This Indo-Burmese dish may be served with any vegetarian dish. My own preference is to serve it with Indo-Burmese lamb dishes, or a curry.

½ cup dried red lentils
3 tablespoons butter or margarine
2 bay leaves
3 whole cloves
1 cup uncooked rice, well rinsed and drained
¼ teaspoon salt
1½ cups water

1. Rinse the lentils, cover with water, and soak for 1 hour. Drain well.

2. Melt the butter in a pan over low heat. Add the bay leaves and cloves and stir for 2 minutes. Add the rice and salt and mix well.

3. Add the water, cover the pan, and bring the mixture to a boil. Cook until the rice is half done, about 5 minutes. Add the lentils, mix well, cover the pan, and cook over low heat for 10 minutes more. Stir once or twice with a fork toward the end of this time.

4. Let the rice and lentils stand, covered, for 10 minutes more before dining.

Serve warm with other dishes.

SERVES 4 TO 6

HTAMIN

Burmese-Style Rice

1 cup uncooked rice, well rinsed under cold water, drained
5 cups water

1. Put the rice and water in a pan, cover, and bring to a boil. Cook over moderate heat for 10 minutes.

2. Drain off the water carefully and reserve it. Return the rice in the covered pan to moderate heat and let it dry out for 2 minutes. Turn the heat to low and let the rice continue to dry out for 5 minutes more. Do not remove the cover at any time during this procedure. Shake the pan back and forth several times so that the rice will not stick to the bottom. The rice will become soft and grains will stay separated.

Serve warm or at room temperature.

SERVES 4

Note: I prefer to let the rice remain covered off the heat for another 10 minutes or more before dining, since that ensures that the grains will be cooked. In my opinion, the flavor also improves.

HTAMIN CHIN

Mashed Rice

Rice has a spongy texture when served this way. For added flavor and texture, sprinkle lightly with Crispy Garlic Slices and Garlic Oil (see Index) or with Fermented Soybeans (Tempe, see Index).

2 cups uncooked rice, rinsed
1 pound ripe tomatoes, about 4, quartered
3½ cups water, approximately

1. Bring the rice, tomatoes, and water to a boil, reduce heat to low, cover the pan, and cook for 12 to 15 minutes. Let stand covered for 10 minutes more.

2. Mash the rice in a food mill or processor while still warm. Do not overprocess so that the rice is reduced to baby food; it should have some texture.

3. Oil the inside of a standard tea cup. Fill it with the mashed rice and press it down firmly. Turn the cup over onto a serving platter. Prepare all the rice this way.

Serve at room temperature with Fish Cakes and Coconut Cream (see Index) or anything else.

SERVES 8

ON THAMIN

Coconut Rice

Coconut rice is rich and flavorful—a dish not for daily use but saved for special occasions. It is customary in most Burmese cities to see street vendors offering their own version of this rice as take-out food.

> *3 cups uncooked rice, well rinsed*
> *4 cups Coconut Milk (see Index)*
> *½ teaspoon salt*
> *1 small onion, quartered, about ¼ cup*
> *1 tablespoon sugar*
> *1 tablespoon corn or peanut oil*

1. Mix everything together in a pan and bring to a boil over moderate heat. Cover the pan and reduce the heat to low.

2. Cook for 18 to 20 minutes. Stir once during the cooking process. If rice becomes too dry before it is cooked, add 1 or 2 tablespoons water.

Serve warm with other dishes, especially meat curries.

SERVES 6

ALOO-HTAMIN NE

Mashed Potatoes and Rice

This is a surprisingly tasty preparation, slightly sticky because of the potatoes. It goes admirably with Burmese spiced dishes, especially meat or brain.

The cup-shaped portions of mashed potatoes and rice may be reheated the next day in a steamer for about 5 minutes. Or you may cut them into ½-inch-thick slices and fry them lightly. They are also good cold, served with salads.

½ pound potatoes, 2 medium-size
1 cup uncooked rice
¼ teaspoon salt
Crispy Garlic Slices (see Index)
Garlic oil (see Index)

1. Cook the potatoes in their skins until soft. Drain and peel. Cook the rice until soft.

2. With a potato masher or a processor mash the potatoes. Add the rice and salt and process or mix together thoroughly. Do not overprocess.

3. Press about ½ cup of the mixture into a lightly oiled tea cup, then turn it over on a serving plate. Do this with all the mixtures.

Serve warm or at room temperature, sprinkled with garlic crisps and a few drops of garlic oil.

SERVES 4

HTAMIN KYAW

Burmese-Style Fried Rice

2 tablespoons corn or peanut oil
⅛ teaspoon ground turmeric
1 tablespoon sliced onion
1 cup Cooked Garden Pea Sprouts (Pepyoat, see Index)
1 large egg, beaten
2 teaspoons fish sauce
½ teaspoon salt
3 cups cold cooked rice

1. Heat the oil in a wok or large skillet and add the turmeric and onion. Fry over moderate heat until the onion is light brown.

2. Add the pea sprouts and stir well. Add the egg, fish sauce, and salt. Stir-fry until the egg has set, about 2 minutes.

3. Add the rice and stir-fry for 2 or 3 minutes to combine all the ingredients.

Serve warm with meat or fish dishes.

SERVES 4

Note: After the egg has set in step 2, the dish may be served as a Garden Pea Sprout and Egg Fry, a complete recipe in itself, to be served as a side dish. Or you may continue by adding the rice.

KABAB KHANA

Fried Rice, Indo-Burmese Style

This is an Indian recipe but has been Burmanized to such a degree—as with most Burmese imports—that it has changed into a Burmese dish. The original of this particular fried rice recipe is sold from the food stalls around Rangoon University campus to hungry students at a most reasonable price.

1 tablespoon corn or peanut oil
⅛ teaspoon ground turmeric
1 small onion, sliced thin, about ¼ cup
2 tablespoons thin-sliced fresh semihot chili
1 egg, beaten
½ cup ¼-inch dice of roast or boiled beef
½ teaspoon ground cuminseed
2 cups cold cooked rice
1 tablespoon soy sauce
½ teaspoon salt
¼ cup loosely packed fresh mint leaves

1. Heat the oil in a wok or large skillet and stir-fry the turmeric and onion over moderate heat for 1 minute. Add the chili and stir-fry for another minute. Add the egg, mix, and stir rapidly for 1 minute. Add the beef and continue to stir-fry. Sprinkle the mixture with the cuminseed.

2. Add the rice, soy sauce, and salt, mix, and stir-fry for 2 minutes. Lastly, add the mint, mix well, and stir for 2 minutes more.

Serve warm with other dishes.

SERVES 4

E-PWANT
Stuffed Rice Sheet Bundle

1 teaspoon corn or peanut oil
¼ cup thin onion slices
2 garlic cloves, chopped
½ inch of fresh ginger, chopped
½ pound pork, ground
1 teaspoon salt
1 teaspoon brown sugar
2 cups shredded cabbage
2 teaspoons soy sauce
1 tablespoon cornstarch, dissolved in ¼ cup cold water
¼ cup chopped fresh celery leaves
2 fresh rice sheets

1. Heat the oil in a skillet and stir-fry the onion, garlic, and ginger over moderate heat for 2 minutes. Add the pork, salt, and sugar and stir-fry until the pork color changes.

2. Add the cabbage and soy sauce and stir-fry for 3 minutes. Pour in the cornstarch mixture and stir-fry for 2 minutes. Stir in the celery leaves. Set the skillet aside.

3. For each bundle, take half of a rice sheet and trim off loose pieces top and bottom to make a rectangle. Put ½ cup of the pork mixture into the center of the sheet and fold the sides over to make a bundle 4 inches square and about 2 inches high. Trim off excess rice sheet if there is more than needed. Continue until all ingredients are used.

4. Steam the bundle in a Chinese-style steamer over hot water for 10 minutes.

Serve warm as a snack. Often served with chili sauce or tomato ketchup at the tea or coffee hour.

MAKES 4 BUNDLES

Note: The excess rice sheet strips can be used in stir-fried dishes with chicken, pork, or shrimp. See Index for the Malay Noodle Stir-Fry.

MON YE PA (YE MON)

Stuffed Rice Pancakes

This interesting and delicious pancake is served by street vendors at the Pagoda Festival in Rangoon during the summer months. In Upper Burma, in village after village, the stuffed pancakes are served throughout the year, and are usually purchased from food stalls rather than prepared at home. They are eaten the same way as Indian bread is eaten, by pulling pieces off the pancake with the fingers.

2 cups rice flour
3 cups cold water
1½ teaspoons salt
¼ cup sesame seeds
1 tablespoon corn or peanut oil
1 cup Cooked Garden Pea Sprouts (Pepyoat, see Index)
2 scallions, sliced thin
Pinch of pepper

1. Mix rice flour, cold water, and ½ teaspoon salt together into a thin batter.

2. Toast the sesame seeds and remaining salt together in a dry skillet over low heat for about 5 minutes, or until the seeds become a light tan color. Grind to a coarse mixture in a blender. Do not overprocess and turn to powder.

3. Rub a 12-inch skillet or pancake griddle with the oil. Pour in ¼ cup (or a bit more) batter, spread it into a 12-inch pancake, and cook over low heat.

4. As the pancake cooks, spread over it 2 tablespoons garden pea sprouts, 1 tablespoon scallions, and 1 teaspoon of the toasted sesame and salt mix. Add a pinch of pepper. Let the open pancake cook for 2 minutes. Fold pancake in half and cook for 1 minute more. The underside of the pancake should be browned, not soft or spongy.

Serve warm as an appetizer or snack with tea, coffee, or drinks.

MAKES 5 TO 7 PANCAKES

BE-OO HIN DOK

Stuffed Egg Pancakes

These elegant Burmese egg rolls are perfect for either a small or large party. They can be made in advance, then browned in a small amount of oil when ready to serve.

PANCAKE

 3 eggs, beaten
 3 tablespoons flour
 2 tablespoons cold water
 ½ teaspoon salt
 2 teaspoons corn or peanut oil

STUFFING

 ¼ pound shrimps, peeled, deveined, quartered
 ¼ teaspoon salt
 1 Chinese tofu cake, cut into 9 cubes, browned in oil, cooled, cut
  into ¼-inch pieces
 1 boiled or fried Basic Fish Cake (Nga Phe Kyaw, see Index), cut
  into ¼-inch cubes
 1 tablespoon chopped fresh coriander
 1 scallion, sliced thin
 1 teaspoon corn or peanut oil

1. Beat all pancake ingredients except the oil together to make a smooth batter.

2. Heat a few drops of oil in a nonstick skillet. Pour in about ⅓ cup of the batter and tilt the pan back and forth so batter covers the surface. Cook the pancake over moderately low heat for 1 minute, or just long enough to make the batter firm. Remove to a flat plate. Prepare all the pancakes this way and set aside.

3. Stir-fry the shrimps with ¼ teaspoon salt in a dry nonstick skillet for 2 minutes.

4. Mix all stuffing ingredients except the oil together. Fill each pancake with an equal portion of the stuffing and roll up, leaving the ends open.

(continued on next page)

5. Heat a few drops of oil in a nonstick skillet. Brown the stuffed pancakes on all sides over moderate heat for 2 to 3 minutes.

Serve warm as an appetizer, using any Burmese dip.

MAKES 5 STUFFED PANCAKES

HTAD-TAYA

100-Layer Pancakes

The 100-Layer Pancake (known in New York as the 1,000-Layer Pancake) is of Indian origin. It is the *parata* transferred to Burma by Indian immigrants and adapted to Burmese taste. The "hundred" layers are formed when each pancake is rolled into a cone and then flattened out before being cooked. These layers give the pancakes added texture and tenderness.

DOUGH
> 5 cups flour
> ½ teaspoon salt
> 2 tablespoons sugar
> 1½ teaspoons baking powder
> 1½ cups water
> 3 large eggs, beaten
>
> 2 teaspoons melted vegetable shortening or corn oil
> 2 teaspoons oil for skillet

1. Sift the flour, salt, sugar, and baking powder into a large mixing bowl. Make a well in the center of the flour.

2. Pour the water and eggs into the well and gradually incorporate the flour into the liquid, mixing it slowly and thoroughly. If the dough is still sticky when all the ingredients have been mixed together, add 1 or 2 tablespoons more flour. Knead the dough for about 10 minutes, or until smooth and manageable. (At this point dough may be wrapped in plastic and refrigerated overnight for use next day.)

3. Cover the bowl and set aside at room temperature for 30 minutes.

4. Knead the dough for 15 minutes more. It should be smooth but still moist and stretchable. Divide the dough into 15 or 16 balls. Cover and set aside until ready to use.

5. On a well-oiled wood or metal surface, press out 1 dough ball with your fingertips to make a round disc 5 inches in diameter.

6. Roll out the disc with a rolling pin to a paper-thin pancake 12 to 14 inches in diameter. Or fling out the disc like a pizza thrower, as many times as needed to reach the required size.

7. Dribble shortening or oil over the pancake and rub it over the surface. Cut a line from the center out to the edge of the pancake. From the cut edge, roll the dough around the circle to shape a solid cone. (This makes the layers.) Stand the cone on its thick end and press the pointed end down, to form a ball. Now press this ball out with your fingertips to make a 5-inch pancake.

8. Heat the oil in a skillet or use a pan with nonstick lining and fry the pancake over moderately low heat for 3 minutes on each side, more if you wish a crisper exterior. The slow frying will also bake the inner pancake leaves. Drain a moment on paper towels. Cut into halves or quarters with scissors.

Serve warm.

MAKES 15 OR 16 PANCAKES

PEA PALATA

100-Layer Pancakes Stuffed with Garden Pea Sprouts

These pancakes are usually served as a side dish but I have had great success in using them, cut into 6 pieces, for an accompaniment to drinks.

STUFFING

> *2 teaspoons corn or peanut oil*
> *⅛ teaspoon ground turmeric*
> *½ teaspoon salt*
> *2 cups Cooked Garden Pea Sprouts (Pepyoat, see Index)*
>
> *Dough for 100-Layer Pancakes (see Index)*
> *1 tablespoon Crispy Fried Onions (see Index)*
> *2 tablespoons corn oil for panfrying*

1. Prepare the stuffing. Heat the oil in a skillet. Add the turmeric, salt, and sprouted peas, and stir-fry over moderate heat for 5 minutes. Set aside until ready to use. Leftover stuffing may be kept in the refrigerator for a week.

2. On a well-oiled wood or metal surface, press the dough ball out with your fingertips to make a round disc of 5 inches.

3. Roll out the dough ball with a rolling pin to make a paper-thin pancake 12 to 14 inches in diameter. Or fling out the disc, like a pizza thrower, enough times to produce the required size.

4. Put ½ cup garden pea sprout stuffing in the center of the pancake. Sprinkle with the onion. Fold the pancake envelope style into a rectangle 4 by 5 inches. Gently press the stuffing out flat so that it touches the inner corners.

5. Heat the oil in a skillet and fry the pancake over moderately low heat for 3 minutes on each side, more if you wish a crisp exterior. Drain for a moment on paper towels.

Cut into halves or quarters with scissors and serve warm.

SERVES 4

AMETHA OR KEEMA PALATA

Beef-Stuffed 100-Layer Pancakes

Although the beef-stuffed pancakes originated in India, they appear in Burma as these *keema palata,* and in Indonesia as the *martabak.* They date back to the Hindu immigrants of the thirteenth century.

Dough for 100-Layer Pancakes (see Index)
Oil or vegetable shortening
1 egg, beaten
2 tablespoons diced onion
1 teaspoon chopped fresh mint
¼ teaspoon ground cuminseed
⅛ teaspoon salt
1 tablespoon corn oil for panfrying

GROUND BEEF STUFFING
1 pound ground lean beef
1 teaspoon salt
½ teaspoon ground turmeric

1. First make the stuffing by stir-frying the beef, salt, and turmeric in a dry pan for 5 minutes, or until beef is cooked. Discard fat and put aside the stuffing until ready to use. Extra stuffing may be kept in the refrigerator for 1 week.

2. On a well-oiled wood or metal surface, press out the dough ball with your fingers to make a disc 5 inches in diameter.

3. You may roll out the disc with a rolling pin to a paper-thin circle 12 to 14 inches in diameter. Or fling out the disc, like a pizza thrower, enough times to produce the required size.

4. Drizzle 2 teaspoons oil over the circle and smooth it evenly over the surface. Spread 2 tablespoons of the egg over all. Sprinkle over that 2 tablespoons beef stuffing, and scatter the onion, mint, cuminseed, and salt over the pancake.

5. Fold all four sides of the pancake over, envelope style, to shape a rectangle 4 inches by 5 inches.

(continued on next page)

6. Heat the oil in a skillet. Add the pancake, folded side down, and brown over moderately low heat until golden, about 6 minutes. Drain on paper towels.

Serve warm, cut into halves or quarters with scissors.

SERVES 4 TO 6

Note: The pancakes may be prepared a day in advance, fried, and then refrigerated. Reheat on a cookie sheet in a 375°F. oven for 10 minutes, or until sizzling. Cut and serve.

PALATA-ACHO

Sweet 100-Layer Pancake

1 crisp-fried 100-Layer Pancake (see Index)
1 to 2 teaspoons sugar
1 tablespoon Coconut Cream (see Index)

1. If you want the pancake to be extra spongy, place a towel on the counter and hold a warm pancake upright on it. Keep turning the pancake and tapping the edges to separate the inner layers. This step is optional.

2. Cut the pancake into 6 wedges, sprinkle with sugar, and spread on the coconut cream.

The sweet pancake is eaten warm or at room temperature, with your fingers, as a dessert or snack at the tea or coffee hour.

SERVES 4

VEGETABLES
AND SALADS

There is a wealth of vegetables available in this great agricultural country, but the garden vegetables most commonly used are the gourds, long beans, chayote, and all the greens of the Chinese cabbage family. Then, too, the Burmese cook has a knowledge of the edible wild plants and herbs. He gathers shoots, leaves, tendrils, and aquatic greens that grow in the fields and rice paddies and with them adds health and interest to his daily diet.

A discussion of the Burmese salad could fill a book by itself. A catchall word, really, their "salad" runs the gamut from a simple condiment to a complex preparation we'd call a one-dish meal. The Dan Bauk Salad (see Index) is a simple matter of some thin-sliced onion, mint leaves, and diced green pepper, while the Special Chicken Salad of the Mon (Kyettha Thoat, see Index) can be served as a hot chicken dish with a soupy lime and chili dressing, or as a main-dish soup. Nowhere will you find the conventional lettuce and tomato combination so prevalent elsewhere.

Perhaps the most unusual of salads is the Lephet—the fermented young tea leaves around which a ritual has been born. We open the chapter with its history.

LEPHET

Fermented Tea Leaf Salad

A CULTURAL PHENOMENON

In the area around the town of Pagan, you will see hundreds of miles of ruins—pagodas and Buddhist temples, one after the other, one more beautiful and exotic than the other—an archaeological treasure. It was here that Alaung Sithu, the most famous king of the Pagan Dynasty, lived and in A.D. 1113 introduced tea into Burma. He imported seeds from China and requested the Palaung tribesmen to grow and harvest the tea. It was here that they first decided to ferment the fresh young leaves, making lephet and starting a habit that developed into a ritual and a great social pastime.

The Burmese are the only people, as far as I know, who eat tea leaves. Tea is a stimulant, and constantly nibbling it helps to keep one awake and alert through long conversational dissertations, plays, puppet shows, dances, or family gatherings. Although one Colonial Englishman referred to *lephet* disparagingly as "pickled tea" which is mixed with "salt, garlic and assafoetida, doused in oil," I like it and find eating it a convivial and social habit. Our Englishman went on to rail against the "overpowering horrors" of asafetida (not used here), which in Colonial days gave *lephet* a bad name.

Unfortunately, the main ingredient—fresh tea leaves—is not available here, but still the recipe is unique and of historical interest, so worthy of inclusion.

The hill tribesmen, especially the Palaung, who have been preparing *lephet* for centuries, collect the young fresh tender tea leaves just before the start of the rainy season. The leaves are steamed just enough to wilt them and then are pressed firm in large bamboo cylinders. The filled cylinders will then be stored in the earth or a cellar. This slightly ferments the leaves and gives *lephet* its characteristic astringent flavor. Now the leaves are ready to eat.

There are two methods of serving *lephet*—the traditional and the modern styles.

Traditionally, *lephet* is served in a round lacquer dish that is divided into sections. Each division contains a different ingredient to accompany the tea leaves. Toasted sesame seeds and Crispy Garlic Slices (see Index) are both indispensable items. Other choices may be roasted peanut halves and tiny dried shrimps. Small dried lima beans, split and fried in oil, are sometimes included.

The diner first kneads his tea leaves with a little salt and oil until they become malleable and places them in one section of the dish. Then he nibbles at this assortment, taking a pinch of tea leaves, a few sesame seeds, and a garlic slice or two. Conversation becomes brisk, the palate is cleansed, and some even say the tea is a digestive.

The second and modern method of serving *lephet* is in a salad. The young Burmese, especially, use this combination to serve at social gatherings. The modern assortment, prepared in small quantities, would include the traditional ingredients:

3 tablespoons lephet
1 teaspoon corn or peanut oil
⅛ teaspoon salt
3 tablespoons toasted sesame seeds
2 tablespoons Crispy Garlic Slices (see Index)

Plus, as optional choices, finely shredded cabbage, ground shrimp powder, ripe but firm tomato strips, lime or lemon juice, sliced hot green chili, and fish sauce. The ingredients are all mixed together by hand, according to personal taste.

PE-WETSI

Cranberry Bean Fry

2 pounds cranberry beans in the shell
3 tablespoons corn or peanut oil
⅛ teaspoon ground turmeric
1 small onion, sliced thin, ¼ cup
1 cup water
1 teaspoon salt

1. Shell the beans and skin each one. The beans that remain will weigh about 1 pound.

2. Heat the oil in a skillet and add the turmeric and onion. Brown onion for about 2 minutes.

3. Add the beans and stir-fry the mixture for 2 minutes. Add the water and cover the pan. Cook over moderately low heat until the beans soften and reduce to a purée. Mix well. At this state add the salt and mix again. The water will have been absorbed and the beans will be puréed.

Serve warm as a side dish.

SERVES 4 TO 6

Note: Cranberry beans are available principally in Italian groceries, but also in many supermarkets. Their attractive but inedible pods are mottled in various shades of pink; the large beans inside have a light beige skin also mottled with pale pink. Skins are tough and so usually are removed before cooking. The bean purée has a most attractive mealy flavor and is popular in Burma. When cooking beans, the Burmese always add salt last. They have found that adding it earlier prevents the beans from cooking evenly.

PETHE KYAW

Stir-Fried Chinese Long Beans

½ pound Chinese long beans
2 tablespoons corn or peanut oil
⅛ teaspoon ground turmeric
1 garlic clove, sliced thin
1 tablespoon thin-sliced onion
1 tablespoon dried shrimp powder
½ teaspoon salt
½ teaspoon fish sauce
¼ cup water

1. Slice the Chinese beans into diagonal pieces about 2 inches long.

2. Heat the oil in a wok or skillet and add the turmeric, garlic, and onion. Stir-fry the mixture over moderate heat for 1 minute.

3. Add the beans, shrimp powder, salt, and fish sauce. Continue to stir-fry for 2 minutes. Add the water and stir-fry until the water has evaporated and the beans are tender but still have texture.

Serve warm or at room temperature with other dishes.

SERVES 4

Note: The Chinese long bean is used in India where it is known as *loobia*. It is also known as asparagus bean. The supermarket snap bean may also be used for this recipe.

PE KYAZAN KYAW

Vegetarian Bean Thread Mix

This is essentially a vegetarian dish and I prefer it that way. However, you may include ½ cup of cooked cubed chicken, pork, or shrimp toward the end of the cooking process if you like, to give it more substance.

> 1 tablespoon corn or peanut oil
> 1 small onion, sliced, ¼ cup
> ¼ pound green snap beans, cut long and thin, diagonally
> 2 cups shredded cabbage
> 4 ounces cellophane noodles, soaked in warm water for 15
>   minutes, well drained
> 2 tablespoons soy sauce
> ½ teaspoon salt
> 2 eggs, beaten

1. Heat the oil in a wok or large skillet and fry the onion over moderate heat for 1 minute. Add the snap beans and stir-fry for 2 minutes. Add the cabbage and stir-fry for 2 minutes more.

2. Now add the noodles, soy sauce, and salt, and stir-fry the mixture for 2 minutes. Push the mixture to the side of the wok, add the eggs, and scramble them. When they begin to set, incorporate them with the rest of the mix.

Serve warm with other dishes.

SERVES 6

PEBYA GAWBI KYAW

Crisp Tofu Cakes and Cabbage

1 pound Chinese cabbage
Oil for deep-frying
2 Chinese tofu cakes, cut into 6 cubes each
2 garlic cloves, chopped
1 tablespoon soy sauce
½ teaspoon sugar
¼ teaspoon salt
½ cup coarse-chopped celery leaves

1. Cut the cabbage into ½-inch-wide slices.

2. Heat the oil in a skillet and brown the tofu cakes over moderate heat on both sides until lightly crisp, about 5 minutes. Remove and set aside. Remove all except 1 tablespoon oil.

3. Heat the oil in the skillet again and brown the garlic for 1 minute. Add the cabbage and stir-fry for 2 minutes, to wilt the slices. Add the tofu, soy sauce, sugar, and salt. Mix well. Finally add the celery leaves and stir-fry for 1 minute.

Serve warm with other dishes.

SERVES 4

Variation: This is a basic recipe, which may be altered in flavor and texture somewhat by substituting other vegetables. Swiss chard is excellent. It would be also be typical to use small cauliflower florets or young broccoli stems cut into 1-inch pieces. The weight and seasonings are the same regardless of the vegetable used.

KAYAN THI HNAT

Stuffed Eggplant

1 pound small eggplants, about 4
3 tablespoons shrimp powder
2 garlic cloves
1 small onion, sliced, ¼ cup
1 teaspoon paprika
1 teaspoon salt
2 tablespoons corn or peanut oil
¼ teaspoon ground turmeric
½ cup water

1. Trim off the stems of the eggplants. Make 2 cuts at right angles into each one, from the top down to 1 inch from the bottom. This will divide it into 4 parts held together at the bottom and will provide a container for the stuffing.

2. In a mortar or food processor crush the shrimp powder, garlic, onion, paprika, and salt to a coarse consistency. Stuff each eggplant with the mixture and push the eggplant back into shape.

3. Heat the oil in a skillet and add the turmeric. Add the stuffed eggplants and over moderate heat fry them for 2 minutes on each side.

4. Add the water and cover the pan. Cook over low heat for 15 minutes until the eggplants are soft and the liquid has nearly all evaporated.

Serve warm with rice as a main or side dish.

SERVES 4

Variations: You may add ⅔ cup cooked ground beef, pork, lamb, or fresh shrimps to the crushed flavoring mixture to enrich the stuffing. In that case you should cook the eggplant for 20 minutes.

KAYAN THI BE OO

Baked Eggplant Purée with Egg

2 pounds eggplant, 1 or 2
½ teaspoon salt
2 tablespoons corn or peanut oil
1 small onion, sliced thin
2 eggs, beaten with 1 teaspoon salt
¼ cup sliced fresh coriander leaves and stems
1 scallion, cut into ¼-inch pieces

1. Grill the eggplant in a broiler or over charcoal until soft, about 15 minutes. Turn several times. Peel and discard the skin and stem. Reserve any eggplant liquid.

2. Mash the eggplant and liquid into a purée. Add the salt and mix. Adjust salt to taste, adding more if needed.

3. Heat the oil in a skillet and over moderate heat fry the onion until crisp and light brown. Remove and set aside.

4. Add the eggplant to the oil and stir-fry over moderate heat for 1 minute. Add the eggs and stir them until they set, about 3 minutes. Lastly, add the coriander, scallion, and half of the crisp onions. Stir a moment.

Serve warm or at room temperature and sprinkle with the balance of the crisp onions.

SERVES 4 TO 6

KHAYAN THI PEBYA

Eggplant and Tofu Purée

This is one of the best of the vegetarian preparations. It has an especially pleasing flavor and texture, and it will enhance any Burmese dining experience.

1 *pound eggplants, 2*
2 *Chinese tofu cakes*
2 *tablespoons corn or peanut oil*
1 *garlic clove, chopped fine*
½ *teaspoon salt*
1 *tablespoon soy sauce*
1 *egg, beaten*
2 *tablespoons chopped coriander*
2 *scallions, sliced thin*

1. Bake the eggplant in an oven or under a broiler for about 15 minutes to char the skin and soften the pulp. Cool and peel. Purée the pulp but not too smoothly.

2. Coarse-chop the tofu.

3. Heat the oil in a skillet and fry the garlic over moderate heat until light brown. Add the eggplant, salt, and soy sauce and stir-fry for 2 minutes. Add the tofu and mix well.

4. Add the egg and stir it into the mixture. Continue to stir-fry for 3 minutes. Sprinkle with the coriander and scallions.

Serve warm as a side dish.

SERVES 4

KYETHINGA

Shrimp-Flavored Bitter Melon

1 pound bitter melon, 1 or 2
½ teaspoon sliced fresh ginger
1 garlic clove, sliced
½ cup sliced onion
2 tablespoons corn or peanut oil
⅛ teaspoon ground turmeric
¼ teaspoon dried hot red chili flakes
½ teaspoon salt
2 tablespoons shrimp powder
¼ teaspoon shrimp paste
2 tablespoons fish sauce
½ cup water

1. Cut the bitter melon lengthwise into halves; scoop out and discard the seeds. Turn over each half and cut into ¼-inch-wide half-moon slices. Rinse them in lightly salted water and drain well. (This removes some of the bitterness.)

2. Coarse-chop the ginger, garlic, and onion. Heat the oil in a wok or skillet and over moderate heat add the turmeric, onion/garlic/ginger, hot chili flakes, and salt. Stir-fry for 3 minutes until the mixture becomes light brown.

3. Add the shrimp powder, shrimp paste, and fish sauce and stir-fry for 2 minutes. Add the bitter melon slices and mix well for 1 minute.

4. Add the water and stir-fry for a minute to combine the ingredients. Turn the heat to low and let the melon cook for 5 minutes, or until it is soft. Do not cover the wok during this procedure or the melon will discolor and turn mushy.

Serve crisp and warm or at room temperature.

SERVES 4

KHAWETHI KYAW-CHET

Ridge Gourd and Shrimp Fry

1 tablespoon corn or peanut oil
1 tablespoon thin-sliced onion
½ cup shrimps, peeled, deveined, cut into ¼-inch pieces
1 teaspoon fish sauce
2 cups peeled ridge gourd slices, ¼ inch wide
1 teaspoon soy sauce

1. Heat the oil in a wok or skillet and lightly brown the onion over moderate heat for 1 minute. Add the shrimp and fish sauce and stir-fry for 1 minute.

2. Add the gourd and soy sauce and stir-fry for 3 to 4 minutes.

Serve warm with other dishes.

SERVES 4

Variation: Zucchini, not peeled, is a good substitute for the ridge gourd if gourd is not available. The texture is firmer but serves well with the shrimps.

PELINMWE

Stuffed Snake Gourd

The snake gourd is a very long cylindrical gourd grown in the tropics. Although common in Burma, it is not available here as far as I know. This recipe may be adapted for green peppers or any other suitable vegetable. (Directions are for green peppers.)

1 medium-size snake gourd, or 4 green peppers, about 1 pound

STUFFING

½ *pound ground beef*
1 *medium-size onion, chopped, ½ cup*
1 *garlic clove, chopped*
½ *inch of fresh ginger, chopped*
½ *teaspoon salt*
¼ *teaspoon shrimp paste*
1 *tablespoon fish sauce*

SAUCE

1 *tablespoon corn or peanut oil*
1 *tablespoon chopped onion*
1 *garlic clove, sliced*
1 *teaspoon fish sauce*
½ *cup water*

1. Cut out the center stem of each green pepper and scoop out the seeds and ribs. Save the stem as a plug.

2. To make the stuffing, mix the beef, onion, garlic, ginger, salt, shrimp paste, and fish sauce together. Stuff the peppers; plug the opening. Set aside.

3. Heat the oil for the sauce in a pan and fry the tablespoon of chopped onion and the sliced garlic over moderate heat for 2 minutes. Add the fish sauce and stir well for 1 minute.

4. Add the peppers to the pan and fry them on all sides for 3 minutes. Add the water, cover the pan, and cook for 20 minutes. Turn the peppers over once during this process.

Serve warm with other dishes.

SERVES 4

KYAUK-YO HMO

Straw Mushrooms and Water Spinach Stir-Fry

We are finding more and more of the hitherto unknown Asian green leafy vegetables in the marketplace because of the influx of people from Vietnam, Thailand, and Cambodia. Water spinach, one of those only now becoming available, is considered by the Burmese to be an antidote for the poisons they believe to be inherent in mushrooms—a favorite vegetable. Therefore, combining spinach with mushrooms is the ideal solution for having your cake and eating it too—safely.

2 teaspoons corn or peanut oil
1 tablespoon sliced onion
½ pound water spinach, leaves and stems, cut into 2-inch lengths
¼ cup ½-inch cubes of sweet red or green pepper
1 teaspoon soy sauce
½ teaspoon salt
1 can (1 pound) straw mushrooms, well drained

1. Heat the oil in a wok or skillet and fry the onion over moderate heat for 2 minutes.

2. Add the water spinach, sweet pepper, soy sauce, and salt, and stir-fry for 2 minutes. Add the straw mushrooms and stir-fry for 2 minutes more.

Serve warm with other dishes.

SERVES 4

HMO HIN

Wild Mushroom Sauté

During the rainy season wild mushrooms are collected all over Burma, while the straw mushrooms are homegrown in sawdust on small farms. This recipe calls for both the wild and the domesticated but full-flavored mushrooms of Burma, and is most successful when one uses a combination of the many varieties of wild mushrooms now available in specialty markets.

> *1 tablespoon corn or peanut oil*
> *2 tablespoons thin-sliced onion*
> *⅛ teaspoon ground turmeric*
> *12 ounces fresh mushrooms, halved, including stems*
> *1 semihot green chili, cut into ½-inch pieces*
> *2 teaspoons fish sauce*
> *½ teaspoon salt*

1. Heat the oil in a skillet and fry the onion and turmeric over moderate heat until light brown, about 2 minutes.

2. Add the mushrooms and chili and stir-fry for 2 minutes.

3. Add the fish sauce and salt. Stir-fry for 5 minutes more to produce a modest quantity of mushroom sauce.

Serve warm or at room temperature with other dishes.

SERVES 4

PEBYA HMWE KYAW

Tofu Mash with Snow Peas

This dish shows its Chinese origin because of the tofu, snow peas, and soy sauce used as ingredients. The Burmese taste influences the finished product as turmeric, paprika (for color), and the individual flavor of cuminseed are added. An admirable blending of two cuisines.

2 Chinese tofu cakes
1 cup snow peas
2 teaspoons corn or peanut oil
1 teaspoon chopped fresh ginger
1 garlic clove, chopped
⅛ teaspoon ground turmeric
½ teaspoon ground cuminseed
1 teaspoon paprika
½ teaspoon thin-sliced fresh hot green chili
2 teaspoons soy sauce
¼ teaspoon salt

1. Coarsely chop the tofu. String the snow peas, rinse well, and refrigerate for 30 minutes to crisp the texture.

2. Heat the oil in a wok or skillet, add the ginger and garlic, and stir-fry over moderate heat for 1 minute. Add the turmeric, cuminseed, and paprika and stir-fry for a minute.

3. Add the snow peas and chili, stir-fry, and then add the tofu, soy sauce, and salt. Mix well, and stir-fry for 1 minute more.

Serve warm with other dishes.

SERVES 4

GAWBI-BOZAPE PEBYAW KYAW

Snow Pea and Cabbage Fry

1 cup snow peas
3 tablespoons corn or peanut oil
2 Chinese tofu cakes, cut into 1-inch squares
1 teaspoon chopped fresh ginger
1 garlic clove, chopped fine
1 cup shredded cabbage
1 tablespoon soy sauce
¼ teaspoon salt
¼ cup water
2 scallions, cut into ¼-inch-wide slices
½ cup ¼-inch slices of celery heart and leaves

1. String the snow peas, rinse well, and refrigerate for 30 minutes to crisp the texture.

2. Heat the oil in a skillet and over moderate heat lightly brown the tofu on both sides. Remove tofu and set aside. Remove all but 2 teaspoons oil.

3. In the same pan, add the ginger and garlic and stir-fry over moderate heat for 1 minute. Add the cabbage and stir-fry for a moment.

4. Add the snow peas, soy sauce, and salt and mix well. Add the water, then the tofu, and continue to fry. Finally add the scallions and celery and stir-fry for 1 minute more.

Serve warm with other dishes.

SERVES 4

HINNUNWE

Spinach Stir-Fry

This is essentially a side dish to be served with other more complex Burmese dishes, but it has substance and should not be overlooked. The Burmese have a traditional verse that cautions us in rhyme: "Do not overcook or squeeze this tender leaf."

1 pound fresh spinach
1 tablespoon corn or peanut oil
2 tablespoons sliced onion
1 garlic clove, sliced thin
2 tablespoons dried shrimp powder
1 tablespoon fish sauce
½ teaspoon salt
2 tablespoons thin-sliced semihot green chili (optional)

1. Rinse the spinach under cold water several times to remove sand. Trim off tough stems. Drain and set aside.

2. Heat the oil and stir-fry the onion and garlic over moderate heat for 2 minutes. Add the shrimp powder and stir for a moment. Add the fish sauce and salt, and stir-fry for 1 minute.

3. Add the chili and spinach, and stir-fry for 3 minutes to wilt the spinach. Stir and toss but do not overcook.

Serve warm with other dishes.

SERVES 4

PEBYA KHA-O

Tofu and Turnip Sauté

1 Chinese tofu cake
3 tablespoons corn or peanut oil
1 small onion, sliced, ¼ cup
1 small rutabaga, peeled, cut into ¼-inch-thick slices, ⅔ cup
¼ cup chopped ripe tomato, fresh or canned
1 teaspoon thin-sliced fresh hot green chili
2 teaspoons soy sauce
¼ teaspoon ground cuminseed
½ teaspoon salt
¼ cup water

1. Cut the tofu into rectangles about 1 inch wide, 2 inches long and ¼ inch thick. Dry them well on paper towels.

2. Heat a dry skillet for 1 minute, then add the oil (this prevents the tofu from sticking). Fry the tofu over moderate heat to a light brown on both sides. Remove and set aside. Remove all but 1 tablespoon oil.

3. Brown the onion in the oil over moderate heat for 2 minutes. Add the rutabaga slices and stir-fry for 2 minutes. Add the tomato, chili, soy sauce, cuminseed, and salt and stir-fry for 1 minute. Add the water, cover the skillet, and cook for 5 minutes.

4. Add the tofu, stir for a moment, cover the skillet, and cook for 3 minutes more.

Serve warm with bread. An excellent side dish for vegetarians.

SERVES 4

Note: Firm vegetables such as chayote and the white turnip with a mauve top can also be used in this preparation. The contrast of the browned tofu and the soft turnip is pleasant to the palate, and the flavorings give it an unusual and distinctive character.

NGAPI LEIN MAR

Raw Vegetables with Spicy Fish Sauce

This is a grand condiment with considerable dimension, using many of the traditional Burmese flavorings. It is sometimes referred to as a "dip," but it is really a thick paste and must be spooned over other foods. Traditionally eaten with an assortment of vegetables.

¼ cup corn or peanut oil
¼ teaspoon ground turmeric
2 garlic cloves, sliced thin
1 medium-size onion, sliced thin, about ½ cup
1 tablespoon dried shrimp powder
1 teaspoon paprika
1 tablespoon shrimp paste
2 tablespoons fish sauce
½ teaspoon salt
¼ cup chopped ripe tomato, fresh or canned
2 fresh hot green chilies, cut into 1-inch pieces
1 scallion, cut into 1-inch pieces
¼ cup 1-inch pieces of fresh coriander, leaves and stems

1. Heat the oil in a wok or skillet. Add the turmeric and garlic and fry over moderate heat until garlic is brown and crisp. Remove garlic and set aside. Add the onion and fry until light brown. Remove onion and set aside.

2. Add the shrimp powder, paprika, shrimp paste, fish sauce, and salt. Add the tomato and stir-fry for 2 minutes.

3. Add the chilies and scallion and stir-fry for 1 minute. Remove wok from the heat and stir in the crisp garlic and onion and the coriander.

Serve at room temperature with a selection of vegetables. Those that require blanching should be well drained, dried on towels, and refrigerated so that they stay crisp although partially cooked.

SERVES 6

Cabbage leaves or small chunks, blanched in boiling water for 2 minutes, drained well.

Carrot sticks about 2 inches long.

Cauliflower florets, blanched in boiling water for 2 minutes, drained well.

Celery, fresh, crisp, young, finger-length pieces.

Chayote, peeled and cut into finger-size pieces, blanched in boiling water for 5 minutes.

Cucumbers, young, unpeeled, but with ends trimmed. Cut into finger-size slices.

Green Snap Beans, ends trimmed, blanched in boiling water for 5 minutes, drained.

Okra, blanched in boiling water for 5 minutes, drained.

PRA-KAMA-PE

Simple Chick-Peas

Just across the Irrawaddy River from Mandalay, near the town of Sagaing, is the well-known monastery of Pra-Kama. There this simple, easy chick-pea dish has become a favorite with the resident monks.

1 pound dried chick-peas
½ inch of fresh ginger, chopped
1½ teaspoons salt
Crispy Fried Onions (see Index), with oil

1. Cover the chick-peas with water and soak them for 8 to 10 hours.

2. Cook chick-peas with ginger and salt over moderately low heat for about 1 hour or until chick-peas are tender and the water has evaporated.

Serve warm as a side dish sprinkled with as much crispy onions and oil as wanted.

SERVES 6

PEPYOAT KYAW

Stir-Fried Garden Pea Sprouts

2 tablespoons corn or peanut oil
⅛ teaspoon ground turmeric
2 tablespoons sliced onion
1 cup Cooked Garden Pea Sprouts (Pepyoat, see Index)
½ teaspoon salt

1. Heat the oil in a skillet and add the turmeric and onion. Stir-fry over moderate heat until onion is brown.

2. Add the peas and salt and stir-fry for 5 minutes, lightly pressing to crush the peas slightly.

Serve warm or at room temperature.

SERVES 4

PEBOK SE KYAW

Crisp-Fried Fermented Soybeans

This is a strongly flavored preparation of the Shan mountain tribes. High in protein, it is used as a garnish on rice or eaten out of hand. Leftovers may be stored in a tightly covered jar in the refrigerator for 1 month. When serving after refrigerator storage, bring to room temperature or, even better, warm up in oven.

3 tablespoons corn or peanut oil
⅛ teaspoon ground turmeric
1 large shallot, sliced
1 teaspoon dried hot red chili flakes
1 cup Fermented Soybeans (Tempe, see Index)
½ teaspoon salt
2 teaspoons soy sauce

1. Heat the oil in a skillet. Add the turmeric and shallot and stir-fry over moderate heat for 1 minute.

2. Add the chili flakes, stir a moment, then add the soybeans, salt, and soy sauce. Stir-fry the mixture for about 15 minutes to brown the beans. The mixture should become dark and quite dry.

Serve warm as a side dish with rice, fish, or meat dishes.

SERVES 4

PEBOK CHET

Fermented Soybean Mix

A most unusual vegetarian dish that nicely displays the flavors and techniques of Burmese cooking.

3 tablespoons corn or peanut oil
1 garlic clove, chopped
1 inch of fresh ginger, chopped
½ cup thin-sliced onion
¼ teaspoon ground turmeric
1 teaspoon dried hot red chili flakes
2 cups Fermented Soybeans (Tempe, see Index)
1 teaspoon salt
2 teaspoons soy sauce
½ cup roasted peanuts, coarse-chopped
1 large ripe tomato, cut into 1-inch cubes
1 semihot green chili, cut into 4 pieces

1. Heat the oil in a skillet and fry the garlic, ginger, onion, and turmeric over moderate heat until brown. Add the chili flakes, soybeans, salt, and soy sauce and stir-fry for 1 minute.

2. Add the peanuts and stir-fry for 2 minutes. Add the tomato and stir-fry for 2 minutes more to cook it down. Add the semihot chili, stir for a moment, and serve.

Serve warm as a side dish.

SERVES 4 TO 6

MARTHPE BAYAKYAW CHET

Nun's Delight

In Sagaing, a famous Buddhist Center, the monks circulate begging their food from pious householders, in contrast to the nuns who prepare their own. This vegetarian dish is a favorite of the nuns, although they omit the coriander, a known sedative, for fear they might drowse during meditation.

1 tablespoon corn or peanut oil
½ teaspoon ground turmeric
1 small onion, crushed to a paste, about ¼ cup
1 garlic clove, crushed to a paste
½ inch of fresh ginger, crushed to a paste
½ teaspoon paprika
½ teaspoon salt
10 Black Gram Puffs (Marthpe Bayagyaw, see Index), torn into 3
   pieces
1 tablespoon soy sauce
1 tablespoon tamarind paste, dissolved in ½ cup water, strained
   through a metal sieve
¼ cup chopped fresh coriander

1. Heat the oil in a skillet. Add the turmeric, onion, garlic, and ginger, and stir-fry for 1 minute. Add the paprika and salt, stir for a moment, then add the gram puffs.

2. Add the soy sauce and tamarind liquid and stir-fry for 2 minutes. Add the coriander and stir-fry for 1 minute. If the mixture appears too dry (it should be just barely moist), add ¼ cup water and stir-fry for another minute or two.

Serve warm with rice with other dishes.

SERVES 6

KYETTHA THOAT
Cornish Game Hen Salad

This is a traditional salad eaten all over Burma. The Cornish hen lends itself very well to this type of salad. The meat and skin are not excessively fat and provide contrasting textures.

1 Cornish game hen, 1½ pounds, halved
2 cups water
¼ cup thin-sliced onion, rinsed under cold water and dried
2 teaspoons fish sauce
2 tablespoons chopped fresh coriander
1 tablespoon lemon juice, or more
2 tablespoons ½-inch cubes of sweet red pepper
2 tablespoons Crispy Fried Onions (see Index)

1. Put the hen and the water in a covered pan and cook over moderate heat for 30 minutes. Drain, cool, and remove the meat. Cut it into ½-inch cubes. Include as much of the skin as wanted, also cubed.

2. Mix the meat and everything else together. Toss the salad well.

Serve at room temperature as a first course.

SERVES 4

KYETTHA THOAT

Chicken Salad with Lemon

1 medium-size onion, sliced thin
1 cup ½-inch cubes of cooked chicken
½ cup ½-inch cubes of cooked chicken livers and gizzard
¼ cup chopped coriander
1 scallion, sliced thin
2 tablespoons ½-inch cubes of red bell pepper
2 teaspoons lemon juice
2 teaspoons fish sauce
½ teaspoon salt
Lemon wedges

1. Rinse the onion slices under cold water. Dry on paper towels.

2. Mix together all the ingredients except the lemon wedges, and toss the salad.

Serve cold or at room temperature, garnished with the lemon wedges.

SERVES 4

ATHE AMYIT THO
Chicken Giblet Salad

This salad is dependent on the combination of different textures and flavors. One of the most important ingredients is the flavored oil in which onion or garlic has been fried crisp.

1 pound chicken giblets (liver, gizzard, heart)
3 cups water
1 teaspoon salt
1 tablespoon lemon juice
2 teaspoons fish sauce
2 teaspoons soy sauce
¼ teaspoon salt
1 teaspoon oil from Crispy Fried Onions (see Index)
*1 small onion, sliced thin, rinsed under cold water, dried on paper
     towel*
2 scallions, cut into ¼-inch-thick slices
2 tablespoons coarse-cut fresh coriander
2 teaspoons thin-sliced fresh semihot green chili

1. Cook the gizzard and heart in the water with 1 teaspoon salt over moderate heat for 15 minutes. Add the liver and cook for 15 minutes more. Drain well. When the giblets are cool, cut them into thin slices.

2. Mix the giblets with all the other ingredients. Toss well.

Serve at room temperature.

SERVES 6

MANDALAY MISHEE

Long Noodle Salad from Mandalay

Perhaps the most complex and unusual salad and pork dish is the Mandalay Mishee. This wonderful salad originated in Mandalay, the seat of the last Burmese kingdom, and it is indeed a royal production. The word *mishee* means "long noodles," so take care when soaking them that you do not break the noodles; they should remain *long*.

There are several separate recipes used for preparing the ingredients for this dish. Since many of them may be cooked and served independently, we are following the instructions for the assembling of the Mishee with the individual recipes required.

1 pound rice noodles (No. 9 size), soaked in very hot water for 8 minutes, drained well
1 recipe Pork Fritters (see recipe following)
12 fried tofu puffs, purchased in Chinatown shops, sliced into 3 pieces each
1 recipe each of Mandalay Sauces (see recipe following)
1 recipe Pork Shreds and Gravy (see recipe following)
½ cup thin-sliced scallions, both green and white parts
½ cup Fermented Mustard Green Pickles (Mon-Nyin Chin, see Index)
½ pound bean sprouts

ASSEMBLING THE MISHEE

1. Put about 1 cup rice noodles in a plate or soup dish.

2. Place on top a piece of fried pork fritter, cut diagonally into ½-inch-wide slices.

3. Place over and around this 3 slices of tofu puff.

4. Sprinkle over all, according to taste, 2 teaspoons Salt-Tasting and Garlic Sauces and a few drops of Hot Sauce.

5. Add a generous portion of pork shreds.

6. Scatter over that 1 tablespoon scallions and a bit of Mustard Green Pickles.

7. Over that sprinkle 1 tablespoon of the gravy from the recipe for Pork Shreds.

8. Toss everything together as you would a salad. (Traditionally the salad is mixed together with the right hand.)

Pork broth, with 2 tablespoons bean sprouts and 1 teaspoon scallions on each serving, is eaten with the salad. Each diner makes his own choice of ingredients when he goes back for a second helping.

SERVES 8 TO 10

PORK FRITTERS (FOR MANDALAY MISHEE)

PORK STRIPS
   1 pound boneless pork shoulder
   ½ teaspoon star anise
   1 teaspoon sugar
   ¼ cup pale dry California sherry

FRITTER BATTER
   1 cup rice flour
   ½ cup wheat flour
   ½ teaspoon salt
   ½ teaspoon baking soda
   1 large egg
   1 cup cold water

1. Cut the pork into 3-inch-long strips, 1 inch wide and ¼ inch thick. Mix with the anise, sugar, and sherry, and marinate in a covered dish in the refrigerator overnight.

2. Mix both flours together with the salt and baking soda.

3. Beat the egg and water together and add it to the flour. Prepare a smooth batter this way.

4. Heat oil in a wok or skillet. Dip the pork strips individually into the batter and fry over moderate heat until crisp and brown. Drain on paper towels.

Note: Besides their use in the Mandalay Mishee, these fritters make excellent appetizers, especially if served with the three Mandalay Sauces.

MANDALAY SAUCES (FOR MANDALAY MISHEE)

SALT-TASTING SAUCE
4 cubes of preserved bean curd
2 tablespoons bean paste
4 tablespoons soy sauce

GARLIC SAUCE
2 tablespoons sliced garlic
1 tablespoon sugar
½ cup white vinegar
1 inch of fresh ginger, chopped
1 teaspoon paprika
¼ cup water

HOT SAUCE
2 tablespoons toasted dried hot red chili flakes
1 tablespoon roasted peanuts
1 tablespoon toasted sesame seeds
1 tablespoon Crispy Garlic Slices (see Index)
2 tablespoons corn or peanut oil, hot

1. For the Salt-Tasting Sauce, mash everything together with a fork or mix in a blender.

2. For the Garlic Sauce, blend everything together in a food processor to make a smooth sauce.

3. To make the Hot Sauce, grind the chili flakes, peanuts, sesame seeds, and garlic together in a food processor. Turn the mixture out into a jar or bowl and pour the hot oil over it. Mix well. Sauce may be stored in a jar with a tight cover and refrigerated.

PORK SHREDS, BROTH, AND GRAVY (FOR MANDALAY MISHEE)

Besides using each of the parts of this recipe for the Mandalay Mishee, you can serve the pork shreds and broth (with scallions and bean sprouts) for lunch. Or a heartier lunch could be made up of the pork shreds and gravy, served with rice.

PORK SHREDS
   5 pounds, approximately, pork shoulder with bone and skin, cut
      into 4-inch pieces
   7 cups water, or enough to cover
   1 tablespoon salt
   1 tablespoon soy sauce

1. Cook everything together in a covered pan over moderately low heat for 3 hours. Keep adding enough water to make up for evaporation so that when the pork becomes tender there will still be 7 cups of broth. Remove the pork and coarsely shred it.

2. Reserve 1½ cups of broth for the gravy. Use the rest as the soup with Mandalay Mishee, each portion garnished with 2 tablespoons bean sprouts and 1 teaspoon scallions.

GRAVY
   2 tablespoons cornstarch
   3 tablespoons cold water
   1 tablespoon soy sauce
   ½ teaspoon sugar
   1½ cups reserved pork broth

Dissolve the cornstarch in the cold water. Add the soy sauce and sugar. Pour this mixture into 1½ cups hot pork broth and stir until smooth.

MANDALAY NANGYI

Rice Noodle Salad with Curried Cornish Game Hen

This salad of hen, rice noodles, and garnishes is a specialty of the city of Mandalay. The word *nangyi* in the title is translated as "thick string," referring to the size of the rice noodles (same thickness as a no. 9 supermarket spaghetti). Because a special chicken broth is always served with it, we have included that recipe here as an integral part of the menu.

CURRY

> 1 Cornish game hen, 1½ pounds, cut into 4 pieces (include the giblets)
> 1 teaspoon fish sauce
> ¼ teaspoon salt
> 2 tablespoons corn or peanut oil
> ½ teaspoon fine-chopped fresh ginger
> ½ teaspoon fine-chopped garlic
> ⅛ teaspoon ground turmeric
> ¼ teaspoon paprika
> 1 small onion, chopped
> ¼ cup chopped fresh or canned tomato
> 1 cup water

> ½ pound thick rice noodles (rice sticks)

GARNISHES

> 2 tablespoons Toasted Chick-Pea Flour (Besan, see Index)
> 1 small onion, sliced thin
> 1 scallion, cut into ¼-inch-wide slices
> ¼ cup coarse-chopped fresh coriander
> Fish sauce
> 1 tablespoon lightly toasted dried hot red chili flakes
> Wedges of fresh lime

1. Marinate the hen with fish sauce and salt for 15 minutes.

2. Heat the oil in a pan and brown the ginger, garlic, turmeric, and paprika over moderate heat for 2 minutes.

3. Add the onion and game hen and brown well for about 10 minutes. Add the tomato and stir-fry for 2 minutes more. Lastly add the water, cover the pan, and cook for 30 minutes, or until the hen is tender.

4. Cool the curry. Remove all the meat from the bones, cut into cubes, and mix with the remaining curry sauce. Slice the giblets.

5. In a large dish, cover the noodles with boiling water and let stand for 15 minutes. Drain well and set aside.

6. Each person helps himself, putting the food on his plate in the following order: first a generous helping of rice noodles and a heaping tablespoon of the hen and sauce. Then sprinkle over that 1 or 2 teaspoons of the *besan*, several slices of onion, scallion, coriander, 2 or 3 teaspoons fish sauce, and a pinch of the hot chili flakes. Each diner mixes his own salad on his plate and squeezes lime juice over all.

Eat at room temperature and help yourself to seconds, mixed to taste.

SERVES 4 TO 6

Variation: The curried hen can also be served on its own with plain rice.

MANDALAY NANGYI SOUP

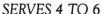

This is the chicken broth always served with the chicken and noodles, Mandalay Nangyi, but one could serve this soup with any kind of Burmese food.

4 cups homemade chicken broth
¼ teaspoon minced fresh ginger
1 small garlic clove, chopped fine
4 whole peppercorns
1 teaspoon fish sauce
2 tablespoons coarse-chopped celery leaves
2 tablespoons sliced scallion

Heat the broth with the ginger, garlic, peppercorns, and fish sauce. Simmer over low heat for 10 minutes.

Serve at room temperature with a garnish of the celery leaves and scallion.

SERVES 4 TO 6

KYETTHA THOAT

Special Chicken Salad of the Mon

The Mon tribe lives in southeast Burma near the border of Thailand. This unconventional salad, credited to them, has a strongly flavored soup dressing and could be either a soup or a salad. Just add more broth to the bowls, if you wish, and serve it as a soup.

BROTH

1 chicken, 3 pounds, quartered, with giblets
6 cups water
3 stalks of lemongrass, halved
1 tablespoon fish sauce
½ teaspoon salt
1 inch of fresh ginger, sliced

SALAD

2 tablespoons thin-sliced green semihot chili
2 tablespoons chopped fresh coriander
2 tablespoons lime juice
2 teaspoons shrimp paste

1. Cook broth ingredients together in a covered pan over moderate heat for 30 minutes. Let stand for 15 minutes more.

2. Remove the chicken and cool. Pull off the meat and discard the skin and bones. Shred the meat; there should be about 4 cups. Strain and reserve 2 cups of the broth.

3. Mix the meat and the 2 cups of broth together and add chili, coriander, lime juice, and shrimp paste. Serve in bowls, while still warm or at room temperature.

SERVES 4

NGA-NITU THOAT

Baby Fish Salad

Dried fish (*nga-nitu*) are a specialty of Arakan (Rakhine) division near the border of Bangladesh. They are exported in some quantities to Southeastern Asian countries, and are available here in Asian food shops. The fish are about 1 inch long. They can be deep-fried in hot oil for a few seconds to make an excellent snack to be served with drinks, as well as being used in this unusual salad.

2 cups water
2 ounces dried baby fish
1 small onion, sliced thin, ¼ cup
1 scallion, sliced thin
1 tablespoon sliced fresh semihot red chili
2 teaspoons Crispy Fried Onions (see Index) with 2 teaspoons oil
1 teaspoon lime or lemon juice

1. Bring the water to a boil, drop the fish in, cover the pan, and cook over moderately low heat for 5 minutes. Drain well.

2. Rinse the onion under cold water and squeeze dry.

3. Mix the fish, onion, scallion, chili, crispy fried onion and its oil, and lime juice. Toss well.

Serve at room temperature with rice and other dishes.

SERVES 4

PAZUN THOAT

Smoked Shrimp Salad

1 pound jumbo shrimps, 10–15 to a pound
1 medium-size onion, sliced thin, rinsed under cold water, drained well
2 tablespoons lemon juice, or more
2 teaspoons Garlic Oil (see Index)
¼ teaspoon salt
2 tablespoons Crispy Fried Onions (see Index)

1. Broil the shrimps in their shells over charcoal or in an oven broiler until lightly charred on both sides. This will provide the smoky flavor. Shell the shrimps and slice them thin.

2. Toss together the shrimps, onion, lemon juice, garlic oil, salt, and crispy onions.

Serve at room temperature.

SERVES 4

Note: Ideally, shrimps should be broiled over charcoal for the maximum smoky flavor. In Rangoon, where I learned this recipe, large fresh shrimps and an outdoor charcoal brazier were easily obtainable and always used.

GAWBI ASEIN THOAT

Fresh Cabbage Salad

> 4 cups fine-shredded cabbage
> 1 cup snow peas, strung and shredded fine
> 4 cups water
> 2 tablespoons dried shrimp powder
> 3 tablespoons fresh lime juice
> 1 tablespoon fish sauce or soy sauce
> 1 tablespoon oil from Crispy Fried Onions (see Index)

1. Cover the cabbage and snow pea shreds with the water. Refrigerate for 2 hours to crisp. Drain very well.

2. Mix the vegetables with the shrimp powder, lime juice, fish sauce, and oil. Toss the salad.

Serve chilled.

SERVES 4 TO 6

Note: For the dedicated vegetarian who will not eat even a trace of fish, substitute soy sauce for fish sauce and peanut powder for shrimp powder. The peanut powder can be prepared by processing ½ cup roasted peanuts.

DUQUADI TO

Cucumber Salad with Toasted Besan

Onions are treated in a special manner when included in salads. The slices are first rinsed under cold water for a moment and then dried on paper towels. The strong onion taste is mellowed but the crunchy texture of the onion remains.

2 cups julienne-sliced unpeeled young cucumber
2 tablespoons ½-inch cubes of sweet red pepper
2 tablespoons Toasted Chick-Pea Flour (Besan, see Index)
2 tablespoons Crispy Garlic Slices with 1 tablespoon Garlic Oil
   (see Index)
1 tablespoon lemon uice
¼ teaspoon dried hot red chili flakes
1 teaspoon fish sauce
½ teaspoon salt
1 small onion, sliced thin (optional)

Toss everything together thoroughly.
Serve chilled or at room temperature with any kind of Burmese food.

SERVES 4

MANGO SALAD

This is the salad traditionally served at New Year's with Water Festival Rice (Thingyan Htamin) and Crisp-Fried Dried Fish (see Index).

1 cup grated unpeeled fresh green mango
1 medium-size onion, sliced, ½ cup
1 tablespoon toasted sesame seeds
½ teaspoon salt
1 teaspoon fish sauce
1 teaspoon dried hot red chili flakes, toasted
1 teaspoon oil from Crispy Fried Onions (see Index)

Mix everything together and toss as one would any salad.

SERVES 4

JIN THOAT

Fresh Ginger Salad

This is an extraordinary salad, to be served in very small quantities at the end of a meal, to indicate that the meal is over. It is flavored with ingredients of unusual character and reflects the Burmese genius for putting it all together. Note that ginger is a digestive.

2 ounces fresh young ginger
Lemon or lime juice to cover, about ⅓ cup
2 tablespoons Crispy Garlic Slices (see Index)
2 tablespoons Toasted Chick-Pea Flour (Besan, see Index)
2 tablespoons sesame seeds, toasted
2 tablespoons fine-shredded sweet potato, fried in hot oil for about
*   1 minute*
2 tablespoons fresh coconut, shredded and fried in hot oil for about
*   1 minute*
2 tablespoons yellow split peas, soaked in cold water for 6 hours,
*   drained and fried in hot oil for about 1 minute*
2 tablespoons roasted skinless peanuts
½ cup thin-shredded cabbage
2 tablespoons shrimp powder
2 tablespoons shrimp sauce
2 teaspoons corn or peanut oil

1. Shred the young ginger (which has a light pink look) into a small bowl and cover it with the lemon or lime juice. Refrigerate for at least 3 days. Then firmly squeeze out and discard the lemon juice.

2. Mix the ginger with all the other ingredients including those that have been toasted and fried.

Serve at room temperature.

SERVES 6 TO 8

YONPADETHI THANAT
Okra Salad

An interesting salad with an unconventional combination of ingredients, yet easy to prepare in the American kitchen.

½ pound fresh young okra
2 cups boiling water
1 tablespoon toasted sesame seeds
¼ teaspoon salt
2 teaspoons fish sauce
1 tablespoon Crispy Fried Onions (see Index)
1 tablespoon roasted peanuts, broken into pieces (optional)

1. Trim off ¼ inch of the stem and tip end of each okra. Drop okra into the boiling water and cook over moderate heat for 2 minutes. Drain well and cool. Cut the okra into ½-inch-wide diagonal slices.

2. Mix the okra with sesame seeds, salt, fish sauce, crispy onions, and peanuts if used. Toss well to mix.

Serve at room temperature with other dishes.

SERVES 4

DAN BAUK SALAD

Usually served with Dan Bauk (Spiced Chicken and Rice, see Index), this salad is a suitable accompaniment to any pork dish or curry.

1 cup thin-sliced onions, rinsed in cold water and dried
½ cup fresh mint leaves
½ cup ¼-inch dice of sweet green pepper
3 tablespoons fresh lime juice
½ teaspoon salt

Mix everything together, adjusting lime juice and salt to taste. Serve.

SERVES 8

LET-THOAT SON

Assorted Vegetable Salad

NOODLES AND VEGETABLES

½ pound fresh egg noodles, cooked in boiling water for 2 minutes, drained well under cold water, set aside

1 pound thin rice noodles, soaked in boiling water for 5 minutes, drained

½ pound cellophane noodles, soaked in boiling water for 3 minutes or longer to soften, drained under cold water, set aside

2 cups cooked rice, mixed with 2 teaspoons hot chili, which colors the rice light pink

1 soft (Japanese) tofu cake, cut into 8 cubes, dried well on cloth towel, deep-fried until brown

2 cups shredded round-head cabbage

2 cups shredded carrots

2 cups boiled potato slices

2 cups bean sprouts, blanched in hot water for 2 minutes, drained well

4 scallions, white and green parts, cut into ¼-inch slices, set aside in 2 heaps

1 cup coarse-chopped fresh coriander

FLAVORINGS

½ cup Toasted Chick-Pea Flour (Besan, see Index)

½ cup dried shrimps, fine-powdered in a processor or coffee mill

2 heaping tablespoons tamarind paste, dissolved in 1 cup water, strained

½ cup Crispy Fried Onions (see Index)

¼ cup Crispy Garlic Slices (see Index), coarsely broken up

¼ cup Garlic Oil (see Index)

Fish sauce

¼ cup dried hot red chili flakes, toasted lightly in a dry skillet

SERVING AND MIXING

Put about 2 heaping tablespoons of each kind of noodle in a plate or bowl. Do the same for rice, tofu, and each vegetable, one on top of the other.

Over all sprinkle 1 teaspoon of each of the flavorings, except the hot chili which is used according to taste. Toss all the ingredients together like a salad, which it is. Dine on this mixture to become acquainted with all the flavors and textures.

The second time around adjust the quantities of everything to suit your preference, a little more shrimp powder, a little less chili, more tamarind liquid, the same with the vegetables and noodles, until you have reached the combination you prefer.

Serve at room temperature.

SERVES 8

Note: *Let-thoat* is a great party salad of many textures and flavors. It means "by hand," that is to say, each diner makes his or her selection and then mixes it with his hand. Burmese tell me that the salad tastes better when eaten out of hand. Traditionally, *let-thoat* is accompanied by a bowl of clear soup with a few leaves of watercress, cabbage, or other green in it.

PAN HTWE PHYAW

Fresh Vegetable Dice

This traditional simple salad uses five different fresh vegetables. It is easily assembled and often served. All ingredients should be chopped into pieces of equal size so that they'll mix well together.

2 large ripe tomatoes, about 1 pound
2 scallions, cut into ¼-inch-wide slices
2 tablespoons thin-sliced semihot red or green chili
⅔ cup ¼-inch-wide pieces of fresh coriander
1 cup diced onion
2 tablespoons fish sauce
½ teaspoon salt
1 tablespoon corn or peanut oil

1. Grill the tomatoes over charcoal or in an oven broiler until the skin is lightly charred. Peel them, cut into quarters, and squeeze out the seeds and liquid. Chop the pulp into coarse pieces.

2. Mix all the ingredients together. Toss well.

Serve chilled or at room temperature.

SERVES 4

KALAPAE THOAT

Chick-Pea and Potato Salad

This salad has substance and flavor that only the unconventional flavorings of Burma supply. The hot chili gives an added zest for those who like it, and the amount may be increased to taste.

2 small potatoes, peeled and halved
1 cup water
1 teaspoon soy sauce
1 teaspoon salt
1 cup cooked chick-peas
1 teaspoon tamarind paste, dissolved in 2 tablespoons water, then
strained
1 scallion, sliced thin
1 tablespoon thin-sliced onion
½ teaspoon ground cuminseed
1 tablespoon coarse-chopped fresh coriander
½ teaspoon dried hot red chili flakes (optional)

1. Cook the potatoes in the water with soy sauce and salt for about 30 minutes, or until they are soft but still firm. Drain well and cut into ½-inch cubes.

2. Mix the potatoes, chick-peas, tamarind liquid, and all the other ingredients together. Toss the salad.

Serve at room temperature with other dishes.

SERVES 4

PEPYACHO THOAT

Grand Tofu Salad

STUFFED TOFU
   2 Chinese tofu cakes
   1 tablespoon rice flour
   1 tablespoon water
   ⅛ teaspoon ground turmeric
   1 cup bean sprouts
   1 cup corn or peanut oil for deep-frying

SAUCE
   ½ inch of fresh ginger, sliced
   1 garlic clove, sliced
   2 heaping teaspoons tamarind paste, dissolved in 2 tablespoons
      water, strained through a metal sieve
   2 teaspoons brown sugar or honey
   2 teaspoons soy sauce
   ½ teaspoon dried hot red chili flakes

SALAD
   2 medium-size onions, sliced thin, about 1 cup
   1 cup julienned young cucumber (sliced in the round, then into
      strips)
   ½ cup fresh coriander, leaves and stems
   2 scallions, sliced thin

1. Cut each tofu cake diagonally into halves. Cut a 3-inch incision in the center of each half, about 1 inch deep or a bit more.

2. Mix the rice flour, water, and turmeric together into a paste. Mix this with the bean sprouts. Stuff each tofu cake pocket with about ¼ cup of the bean sprouts.

3. Heat the oil in a wok or skillet and place the 4 tofu cake halves, cut edge down, in the oil and fry over moderate heat for 2 minutes. Then brown all around for about 4 minutes. Remove tofu cakes and set aside.

4. Rinse the onions under cold water for a moment, lightly squeeze, and dry on paper towels.

5. Cut the fried tofu cakes into 3 pieces. Arrange the salad ingredients into separate piles on a flat place, bean cake in the center surrounded by the onion, cucumber, coriander, and scallion.

6. Crush the ginger and garlic in a mortar into a smooth paste. Mix with the tamarind liquid, sugar, soy sauce, and hot chili flakes. Mix well. Pour the sauce over all. Mix the salad together at the table and toss it lightly.

Serve at room temperature.

SERVES 4

Note: You may increase the hot chili flakes in the sauce according to personal preference.

PEBYA THOAT

Fried Tofu Salad

This simple salad uses all the standard ingredients of a Burmese kitchen. The use of *besan*, shrimp powder, and shrimp sauce as flavorings, along with chili and crisp-fried onions, stamps any dish as authentic Burmese.

2 Chinese tofu cakes, halved
1 medium-size onion, sliced thin, ½ cup
1 tablespoon fish sauce
2 teaspoons dried shrimp powder
2 teaspoons Toasted Chick-Pea Flour (Besan, see Index)
2 teaspoons Crispy Fried Onions (see Index)
½ teaspoon dried hot red chili flakes, lightly toasted
1 tablespoon lime juice

1. Deep-fry the tofu halves until brown. Set aside. Rinse the onion under cold water and dry on paper towel.

2. Cut the tofu into ½-inch-thick slices. Mix all the ingredients together and toss to mix into a salad.

Serve at room temperature with other dishes.

SERVES 4 TO 6

PE PIN PAUK

Bean-Sprout and Tofu Salad

This salad is not only healthful but also has plenty of taste and texture.

2 garlic cloves, sliced
½ teaspoon paprika
1 tablespoon lemon juice
1 tablespoon water
1 teaspoon soy sauce
½ teaspoon sugar
½ teaspoon salt
¼ cup corn or peanut oil
1 Chinese tofu cake
1 small onion, sliced thin, about ⅓ cup
1 pound fresh bean sprouts

1. Mix the garlic, paprika, lemon juice, water, soy sauce, sugar, and salt into a smooth paste in a processor.

2. Heat the oil in a wok or skillet and over moderate heat brown the tofu on both sides. Remove, cool, and cut into 9 cubes.

3. Add the onion to the oil and fry it over moderate heat until light brown and crisp. Remove onion and drain on paper towel.

4. Blanch the bean sprouts in boiling water for 5 seconds. Drain immediately and cool.

5. Mix the bean sprouts, tofu, and sauce together. Toss well to mix. Sprinkle with the crisp onion slices.

Serve at room temperature.

SERVES 4

SWEETS

If you should drop in to visit a Burmese friend some evening, you would probably be offered a cup of green tea and a sweet. Burmese hospitality demands this gracious gesture. And just because it is a gesture, not a meal, there would be two or three choices, perhaps, but very small portions.

The Burmese sweets are not dessert and should not be used as such. We might find them a bit cloying and be satisfied with just a taste.

The Burmese would end their meals with a serving of Fresh Ginger Salad (Jin Thoat), which they consider a digestive, or with the ritual of the Fermented Tea Leaf Salad (Lephet, see Index). I usually offer sherbet or fresh, ripe tropical fruit at the end of a Burmese meal, or even a combination of the two.

KYAUK KYAW

Coconut Agar-Agar Fudge

This fudge looks like marble. The coconut rises to the top and the translucent agar-agar settles on the bottom, resulting in a two-layer sweet.

4 cups agar-agar, about 1 ounce, cut with scissors
5 cups warm water
2 cups sugar
⅛ teaspoon salt
2 cans (12 ounces each) coconut milk, 3 cups

1. Mix the agar-agar and water. Cook the mixture over moderate heat for about 15 minutes, stirring constantly. This will dissolve the agar-agar.

2. Add the sugar and salt; stir to dissolve. Add the coconut milk and cook in an uncovered pan over moderate heat for 30 minutes. Stir frequently.

3. Pour the fudge into a rectangular glass dish about 9 inches square and 2 inches high. Allow the fudge to solidify at room temperature, then cover the dish and refrigerate. Fudge will stay fresh and moist for several days if you cover the fudge with about ½ inch of cold water. Cut into whatever size cubes you wish and serve cold or at room temperature.

MAKES ABOUT 24 PIECES

NATPYEW THI PAUNG

Bananas in Coconut Milk

¼ *cup sugar*
3 cups Coconut Milk (see Index)
5 large bananas, ripe but still firm

1. Mix the sugar and coconut milk together. Cut the bananas lengthwise into halves, put them in a skillet, and pour the coconut milk over them. Bring to a boil and cook over moderate heat for 15 to 20 minutes.

2. Turn the bananas over now and then so that they are well cooked and absorb the coconut milk. Cover the skillet for 5 minutes during this procedure. The oil will separate and some of the liquid evaporate, leaving a thick coconut cream. Skim off and discard the oil.

Serve warm with the coconut cream as a dessert snack with tea or coffee.

SERVES 6 TO 8

Note: Brown sugar may be used in place of white sugar to give a more caramel-flavored sauce.

SHWE GYI SA-NWIN MAKIN

Semolina Sweet in Coconut Cream

In India, where this famous dessert originated, semolina is called *soojee* (and in the United States, Cream of Wheat), and the dessert itself is called *halwa*. The Burmese version is much richer than the Indian one—with added coconut cream, eggs, oil, and sugar—and is delectable. Notice that white poppy seed is used in place of the more common (to us) dark seeds.

> ½ *cup raw peanuts*
> 2 *cups semolina (soojee or Cream of Wheat)*
> 2 *cups sugar*
> 2½ *cups fresh Coconut Cream (see Index) or canned*
> ½ *teaspoon salt*
> 2 *eggs, beaten*
> 3 *cups water*
> ½ *cup corn or peanut oil*
> ½ *cup raisins*
> 2 *tablespoons white poppy seeds*

1. Soak the whole, raw (unroasted), skinless peanuts in warm water for 30 minutes. Drain well and cut the peanuts into slivers.

2. Toast the semolina in a dry skillet, stirring continuously over moderate heat until light brown, 2 to 3 minutes.

3. Mix the semolina, sugar, coconut cream, salt, eggs, water, and oil together in a pan. Mix well and let stand for 30 minutes.

4. Bring to a boil and cook over moderately low heat for about 20 minutes, stirring continuously, until the mixture comes away from the sides of the pan. Stir in the raisins at this time.

5. Put the mixture into a rectangular flameproof dish and smooth the surface. Sprinkle the peanuts and then the poppy seeds over all.

6. Place the dish in a broiler and brown the top for about 3 minutes to toast the peanuts and poppy seeds.

Serve at room temperature as a dessert with tea or coffee.

SERVES 8 TO 10

KHAW PYIN

Sesame Rice Chew

1 cup glutinous rice
2 cups cold water
2 tablespoons toasted sesame seeds
½ teaspoon salt
Oil

1. Soak the rice in the cold water for 30 minutes. Cook together in a covered pan over moderate heat for 15 minutes. Process the cooked rice to a smooth paste.

2. Oil a flat round pan, such as a pizza or pie pan. Spread the rice over the pan and smooth the surface.

3. Grind 1 tablespoon sesame seeds in a processor. Mix the powder with the other tablespoon of the whole seeds and the salt. Sprinkle the mixture over the surface of the rice. Cut the rice into 2-inch squares.

Serve the Rice Chew at room temperature, with or without Sour Cream Sauce or Sugar Syrup (recipes follow), depending on your preference.

MAKES ABOUT 16 PIECES

SUGAR SYRUP
Cook together 1 cup palm sugar and ¼ cup water for about 5 minutes to dissolve the sugar and thicken the syrup. Cool and store in a jar in the refrigerator.

SOUR CREAM SAUCE
Add 2 tablespoons of the Sugar Syrup to ½ cup dairy sour cream.

HTAMANE

Festival Sticky Rice

Htamane is a festival sweet, prepared and served in villages at the rice harvest time, which occurs in winter during the astrological sign of Aquarius (January-February). Its preparation is an arduous bit of work that requires the services of strong men. Pushing, pulling, twisting, stirring the rice, they look like so many athletes wrestling over the huge caldrons. But when the mixture is reduced to a purée of rice, peanuts, sesame seeds, and coconut, and is served to the villagers with a cup of green tea, it is acknowledged to be worth the struggle.

2 cups glutinous (sticky) rice
¾ cup water
1 teaspoon salt
⅓ cup corn or peanut oil
1 teaspoon fine-sliced fresh ginger
½ cup roasted peanuts
⅓ cup toasted sesame seeds
¼ cup thin-sliced coconut, pieces 1 inch long

1. Rinse the rice well in cold water, then cover with water and soak for 1 hour.

2. Drain rice, then add ¾ cup water and the salt. Set aside.

3. Heat the oil in a wok or large pan. Add the ginger and fry for a few seconds. Add the rice and water, and stir well while cooking the mixture over moderately low heat for 1 minute. Cover the wok or pan and let the rice cook for 30 minutes. Stir several times during this process from the bottom to top of the pan. Test by taste to see if the rice has softened.

4. At the end of the cooking time let the rice stand for 10 minutes more off the heat. Then process the rice in a food processor to an almost smooth purée.

5. Finally add the peanuts, sesame seeds, and coconut and fold them into the rice. Spread on a platter and serve warm or at room temperature.

This is a substantial snack traditionally served with green tea.

MAKES 2 DOZEN PIECES

Note: The *htamane* may be refrigerated for several weeks in a plastic container. Warm lightly before serving.

MONPETOK

Sweet Rice and Coconut Pyramids

2 cups glutinous rice flour
1 cup standard rice flour
1½ cups water
⅛ teaspoon salt
1 cup coconut flakes
2 tablespoons sugar
Oil
Banana leaves or aluminum foil

1. Prepare a dough by mixing both rice flours, the water, and salt together. Knead briefly and set aside for 15 minutes.

2. Mix the coconut and sugar together to prepare a stuffing.

3. Pinch off about ¼ cup of dough for each pyramid and flatten it in the palm of your hand. Place 1 heaping tablespoon of the coconut stuffing in the center and fold the dough into a pyramid shape.

4. Rub oil on your fingers and on the inside of the banana leaves or the foil. Wrap a leaf around each rice pyramid and fasten at the top with a wooden skewer. If you use foil, just twist it together at the top. Steam in a Chinese-style steamer over hot water for 30 minutes.

Unroll and discard the wrapper. Eat warm as a snack with coffee.

MAKES 6 TO 8 PYRAMIDS

MON LON YE PAW

Floating Rice Balls

The floating rice balls are served at happy social occasions or gatherings. Many people participate in making them—mixing the dough, cutting the palm sugar, and doing the cooking—and even more wait hungrily for the moment when the balls float to the top and are ready to be served.

2 cups glutinous rice flour
¾ cup standard rice flour
½ teaspoon salt
¾ cup cold water
Palm sugar (jaggery), cut into ¼-inch cubes
Freshly grated coconut

1. Mix both rice flours, the salt, and ¾ cup water together to prepare a smooth rice dough.

2. Take 1 heaping teaspoon of the dough for each ball. Push a hole into it and put in 1 or 2 small cubes of palm sugar. Roll the ball around to enclose the sugar cubes.

3. Bring 6 to 8 cups of water to a rolling boil. Drop the balls into the water, cover the pan, and cook for about 10 minutes. When the balls float, they are cooked.

Remove rice balls with a slotted spoon and sprinkle generously with grated coconut.

Serve warm.

MAKES MORE THAN 50 BALLS

Variations: Take an egg-size lump of dough, and flatten it out to a layer ¼ inch thick. Stuff with 1 heaping teaspoon of Sugared Coconut (see Index). Fold the dough over the stuffing and roll into a ball. Cook the ball in the boiling water for 15 minutes, or until it floats. Remove from the pan and cut open crosswise to reveal coconut. Spread with 1 or 2 teaspoons Coconut Cream (see Index).

The floating balls can be deep-fried in a wok or skillet over moderate heat for about 5 minutes, and drained on paper towel. They are then called *Mon Lon Gyi Kyaw*.

MENUS

Small Party Menus

Small parties or family dining with 4 to 6 persons can still be an adventure if handled with care. Dining for one or two in the comfort of one's home can also be exhilarating. For a cuisine that is relatively unknown, but is a spectacular mixture of India and China, I suggest the following menus. All the menus could be or should be served with plain cooked or coconut rice. For dessert, have fresh or canned tropical fruit. Green tea is served throughout the meal.

1. VEGETARIAN:

Kayan Thi Be Oo, *Baked Eggplant Purée with Egg*
Pe Pin Pauk, *Bean-Sprout and Tofu Salad*
Kalapae Thoat, *Chick-Pea and Potato Salad*
Hmo Hin, *Wild Mushroom Sauté*

2. SEAFOOD:

Nga Phe Kyaw, *Basic Fish Cake, an appetizer*
Pazun Sinkaw, *Chopped Shrimps in Lime Sauce*
Nga Hin, *Simple Fish Curry*

3. SPICY:

Penilay Hincho, *Red Lentil Soup*
Athalon Hin, *Meatball Curry*
Kyauk-Yo Hmo, *Straw Mushrooms and Water Spinach Stir-Fry*
Nga Yok Chin, *Red Chili Dip, a condiment*

4. COCKTAILS AND SNACKS:

Pazun Gwet Kyaw, *Shrimp and Bean-Sprout Fritter*
Payagyaw, *Spiced Yellow-Pea Fritter*
Ngapi Chet, *Anchovy Dip, with assorted vegetables to dip*

5. SPECIAL PARTY:

Pazun Hin Cho, *Clear Shrimp and Lime Soup*
Kyettha Lon Cho Chin, *Chicken Balls in Sweet Tamarind Sauce*
Pethe Kyaw, *Stir-Fried Chinese Long Beans*
Natpyew Thi Paung, *Bananas in Coconut Milk*

6. SUBSTANTIAL DINING:

Side Pau Be-Oo Kyaw, *Omelet with Pickled Turnip*
Wetthani Hin, *Red Pork Pot Roast*
Pan Htwe Phyaw, *Fresh Vegetable Dice*
Shwe Gyi Sa-Nwin Makin, *Semolina Sweet in Coconut Cream*

BIG PARTY MENUS

There are a number of classic Burmese preparations that lend themselves, naturally, to large or moderate gatherings in American homes. The frequent entertainer who is also adventurous in order to expand culinary possibilities will welcome these outstanding Burmese traditional dishes, especially because they are little known outside of Asia. Here is my list of suggested menus for 10 to 12 persons. Multiples of these recipes, judiciously planned, would serve as many as you wish, up to 30 or 40 persons.

1. ON NO KYAUK SWE, *Chicken Curry with Coconut Milk Gravy and Garnishes*

This has everything. A boneless chicken curry in a rich and unusual gravy, served with fresh egg noodles, crispy fried noodles, plus several other garnishes. An important side dish would be the Athe Amyit Hin, Chicken-Liver Appetizer.

To round out what is essentially a buffet presentation, a fine salad, Pe Pin Pauk, Bean-Sprout and Tofu Salad, will provide texture and a perky seasoning.

2. DAN BAUK, *Spiced Chicken and Rice*

Chicken or Cornish game hen, marinated and combined with spiced rice, green peas, raisins, and more ingredients. This Indo-Burmese dish is really a one-dish meal, but it has two major ingredients (chicken and rice) and should be prepared in generous quantities.

A compatible salad suggested to accompany the Dan Bauk is Gawbi Asein Thoat, Fresh Cabbage Salad. In addition, Balachong, Dried Shrimp Garnish, would enhance the presentation.

3. AMETHE LON ALOO, *Meatballs and Potatoes*

There is more to this grand meat and potato dish than meets the eye. It is a combination that has universal appeal and can be assembled for any large number of guests. Along with the presentation of the Amethe Lon Aloo are recommended:

Htamin Kyaw, *Burmese-Style Fried Rice*
Pepyacho Thoat, *Grand Tofu Salad*
Hinnunwe, *Spinach Stir-Fry*
Khayan Chin Thi Ngapi Chet, *Tomato Chutney*

4. MANDALAY MISHEE, *Long Noodle Salad from Mandalay*

Pork is the predominant meat in this mix and match family get-together production. In order to derive the most enjoyment from the Mishee, one should ideally prepare all of the steps including the meat, fritters, sauces, and vegetables. It is a complete, festive meal for entertaining.

5. LET-THOAT SON, *Assorted Vegetable Salad*

The complete vegetarian salad of great dimension, featuring several kinds of noodles, tofu, five vegetables, an assortment of traditional flavorings, toasted dried hot chili to taste, all tossed together in an exotic combination. Easy to assemble.

BIBLIOGRAPHY

Brooklyn Botanic Garden. "Oriental Herbs and Vegetables," *Brooklyn Botanic Garden Record*, Vol. 39. Brooklyn, N.Y.: Brooklyn Botanic Garden, 1983.

Desai, W. S. *India and Burma*. Calcutta, India: Inland Printing Works, 1954.

Dhammananda, K. Sri. *What Buddhists Believe*. Kuala Lumpur, Malaysia: Buddhist Missionary Society, 1982.

Din, U Aung. *The Book of Body Chemistry*. Rangoon, Burma: privately printed, 1977. (Written in Burmese, *Aw-La Rika Thu Khu Ma*, paper.)

Din, U Aung. *Cause and Effect of Body Chemistry*. Rangoon, Burma: privately printed, 1979. (Written in Burmese, *Kyo Kyaung Set Dhat Kyam*, paper.)

Insight Guides. *Burma*. Englewood Cliffs, N. J.: APA Productions, Prentice-Hall, Inc., 1984, paper.

Khaing, Mi Mi. *Cook and Entertain the Burmese Way*. Ann Arbor, Mich.: Karoma Publishers, Inc., 1978, paper.

Kornfield, Jack. *Living Buddhist Masters*. Boulder, Colo.: Prajna Press, 1983, paper.

Masefield, G. B., Wallis, M., Harrison, S. C., and Nicholson, B. E. *The Oxford Book of Food Plants*. Oxford, England: Oxford University Press, 1969, 1975.

Rosengarten, Frederic, Jr. *The Book of Spices*. New York: Jove Publications, Inc., 1981 (c. 1973), paper.

Scott, Sir James George. *The Burman, His Life and Notions by Shway Yoe*. New York: W. W. Norton and Co., 1963, paper. (First edition, London: Macmillan & Co., 1882.) This book by Scott is the most important book on the Burmese people, and is a classic.

United Nations Development Program, Trade Information Service. *Burma Trade Guide, 1984–85*.

INDEX